VCs OF THE FIRST WORLD WAR

THE
SOMME

VCs OF THE FIRST WORLD WAR

THE
SOMME

GERALD GLIDDON

Budding
BOOKS

A Budding Book

First published in 1991 by Gliddon Books, Norwich

First published in this edition in 1994 by
Alan Sutton Publishing Ltd, an imprint of Sutton Publishing Limited

Reprinted 1995

This edition published in 1997 by Budding Books, an imprint of Sutton Publishing Limited,
Phoenix Mill · Thrupp · Stroud · Gloucestershire

British Library Cataloguing-in-Publication Data

A catalogue record for this book is available from the British Library.

ISBN 1-84015-007-6

Library of Congress Cataloguing-in-Publication Data applied for.

Printed and bound in Great Britain by
WBC Limited, Bridgend.

Contents

Preface

This book grew out of my earlier book on the battle of the Somme called *When the Barrage Lifts* in which all fifty one Somme V.C.s make a brief appearance.

I decided to explore the lives of this group of men who won for themselves the highest award for gallantry that their country could bestow. I wanted to try and find out what sort of men they were, and also if they survived the war, what sort of lives that they led after it was over.

The first place to start was with the Canon Lummis collection of material on the lives of all V.C. holders, which is held at the National Army Museum under the stewardship of the Military Historical Society. Although these files are by no means complete they do point researchers in the right direction. I wrote to all the regiments associated with the men and to all the local newspapers in their home towns. I contacted the Imperial War Museum, Commonwealth War Graves Commission and Public Record Office in addition to the appropriate agencies in Canada, Australia, New Zealand and South Africa. I also, of course, read all that I could get hold of about the lives of these men that had been already published.

I have only set out to write a biographical portrait of each man and not a full blown life story and the average entry is roughly 1250 words. I have tried to expand on all previous biographical accounts and in most cases I have written more than has been published before. However, at least four of the men have had whole books devoted to them, ie Congreve, Carton de Wiart, Freyberg, and Bradford. Each section begins with the appropriate action in 1916 when the deed for which the Victoria Cross was awarded took place and then the story reverts to the soldier's early life.

I have listed my main sources at the back of the book under bibliography and appendices. The bibliography covers all the men that I have written about and the appendices give some details of where I obtained much of the rest of the information.

The maps used in the text are based on the map of the Battle of the Somme that was issued with Sir Douglas Haig's Despatches in 1919. The illustrations are acknowledged in the captions as they appear in the text.

I would be very grateful to hear from any reader who may have any suggested corrections to make or who might have additional information.

Acknowledgements

I would like to thank the following institutions and individuals for their very kind co-operation and assistance during the preparation of this book: Australian National Memorial Canberra, Commonwealth War Graves Commission, Gallahers, Imperial War Museum, National Archives of Canada, National Army Museum, Public Record Office, and the Western Front Association. Lady Joan Carton de Wiart, Richard Denyer, Denis Pillinger, Steve Snelling, Tony Spagnoly, Martin Staunton, Ian Uys, and Bob Wyatt. As with my previous book I also owe a very great deal to Winifred my wife who has at all times been supportive.

Also by Gerald Gliddon

When the Barrage Lifts – A Topographical History of the Battle of the Somme 1916

Norfolk & Suffolk in the Great War (Ed.)

Introduction

The Battle of the Somme began on July 1st 1916 after a seven day Allied bombardment. Fourteen British Divisions climbed out of their trenches on an eighteen mile front to the north of the River Somme and advanced slowly on the strongly held German positions. By the end of that day the advance had failed almost everywhere except for small gains at the southern end of the battlefield. There were fifty seven thousand casualties on that disastrous first day and by November 18th, when the battle officially ended nearly a million men from the Allied and German Armies had become casualties.

The Victoria Cross was instituted in 1856 and is still made from Russian cannons captured at Sebastopol. The medal weighs 430 grams and is one and a half inches square.

During the Great War no less than 634 awards of the V.C. were made, of which 51 were for the battle of the Somme. The spread of ranks who won the medal is a fairly wide one, with 20 going to officers, 12 to non-commissioned officers, and 19 going to Privates or their equivalent. In order to qualify for a medal it was of course very important to be seen carrying out the deed itself. No doubt there were many equally deserving cases when a man deserved a Victoria Cross, yet went unrewarded. However I have no qualms about the merits of the Somme V.C. holders; although it is true to say that many of the men did not feel themselves justified in accepting such a high honour when they had seen similar acts of bravery performed around them on the battlefield.

Many of the awards were for the saving of life and not just for rushing forward with a machine gun and spraying it over an enemy held trench in the heat of battle. Indeed many V.C. winners did both, ie killed Germans and saved their compatriots' lives in equal measure. Surely the most heroic figure was Billy McFadzean who in smothering some grenades that had spilt their pins truly gave his life for those of his friends? On the other hand it can be argued that no battle could possibly be won if the momentum was to be continually interrupted by the saving of the lives of casualties. As the Somme battle progressed the job of saving lives was reserved for the stretcher bearers who accompanied the advance or battle.

I am not going to speculate here on the meaning of bravery and where a line can be drawn between heroism and foolhardiness, all I will say is that valour and personal sacrifice are two of the good things that come out of any war.

A third of the Somme V.C.s were awarded posthumously and only 33 survived the war. If the V.C. holder survived then very often he received a considerable amount of what was probably unwanted publicity. He was often invited back to his home town by the local council who then presented him with gifts or an Illuminated Address etc. Some men were also given a gift of money until the War Office cracked down on the practice. It is difficult not to regard all this local attention as an exercise in exploitation and one that helped to encourage local belief in the war effort and in turn help with industrial output in the form of munitions etc. There are many photographs of men who have won the V.C. looking downright embarrassed by the whole business.

The winning of the coveted award also brought other problems in that each man was marked out as something special and if he digressed then it would almost certainly be written up by the press, ie Cunningham and Kelly. Others too, could never settle down after the war although the award of the V.C. could not be given as the reason but rather the war itself. Allen's health was permanently destroyed and he had to resort to alcohol and opium, Hughes took to the bottle, O'Meara never regained his sanity, Cunningham beat up his wife and McNess committed suicide.

On the other hand several men seemed almost to qualify for the award of the medal as if by right, men such as Carton de Wiart, Congreve, Bradford and Freyberg were all brilliant and coura-

geous soldiers. It would surely only be a matter of time before they qualified for the highest of military honours? Others had no problems with the medal and took its ownership in their stride, I am thinking here of men like Adlam, White and Ryder. 'Todger Jones' who rounded up 102 Germans single handed even had correspondence with a film company based on Wardour Street who had plans to make a film out of the heroes of the Somme. He wasn't expecting to co-operate without payment either!

I cannot pretend to have got 'inside' every man that I have attempted to write about and only a fuller biography could achieve this. This book is meant to be a biographical portrait of the 51 men who won the Victoria Cross on the Somme and I am afraid that all too often readers will be left to guess the inner man from the external circumstances. I only hope that I have left enough clues.

E. N. F. Bell

For their attempts to capture the Schwaben Redoubt to the north of the German fortress village of Thiepval the 36th (Ulster) Division were awarded four Victoria Crosses. Three of these awards were given for saving life and one for helping with the attack. The deeds and heroism of the Irish Battalions have gone down in the history books as one of the finest achievements of what turned out to be a day of disaster for the British Army that had no parallel with previous campaigns.

Bell was a temporary Captain with the 9th Royal Inniskilling Fusiliers and on

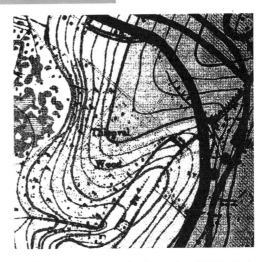

Gallahers Cigarette Card

July 1st was attached to the 109th Bde Trench Mortar Battery. His citation appeared in the *London Gazette* of September 26th and tells the story of how he gained the V.C.:

"For most conspicuous bravery. He was in command of a Trench Mortar Battery, and advanced with the infantry in attack. When our front line was hung up by enfilading machine gun fire Captain Bell crept forward and shot the machine gunner.

Later, on no less than three occasions, when our bombing parties, which were clearing the enemy's trenches, were unable to advance, he went forward alone and threw Trench Mortar bombs among the enemy. When he had no more bombs available he stood on the parapet, under intense fire, and used a rifle with great coolness and effect on the enemy advancing to counter-attack.

Finally he was killed rallying and reorganising infantry parties which had lost their officers.

All this was outside the scope of his normal duties with his battery. He gave

Thiepval July 1st 1916

his life in his supreme devotion to duty."

His body was never found and his name appears on the Thiepval Memorial (Pier and Face 4D and 5B). He was twenty years of age.

———

Eric Norman Frankland Bell was born at Alma Terrace Enniskillen, County Fermanagh, Northern Ireland on August 28th 1895. He was the youngest of three sons of Edward Henry Bell and of Dora Algeo Bell (nee Crowder) . When Eric was born his father was serving with the 2nd Royal Inniskilling Fusiliers at Thayetmyo, Burma as Lieutenant Quartermaster. When the Battalion returned the family were reunited in Warrington, Cheshire. Eric began his education at an Elementary School called the "People's College" in Arpley Street, Warrington.

When the family moved they settled at 114, Huskisson Street in Liverpool. On August 18th 1902 Eric joined St Margaret's School in Liverpool. The family moved to 18 Prince's Avenue, Toxteth and later to 22, University Road, Bootle. Bell moved to the Liverpool Institute and then to Liverpool University where he began to train for a career in Architecture under the eminent Professor Sir Charles Reilly. He was apparently a student whose progress was rapid and he was a keen musician as well as linguist. He was described as being reserved and unpretentious.

On the outbreak of war he joined the Inniskilling Fusiliers as a Second Lieutenant on September 22nd 1914 and was posted to the 6th Battalion. He was 19 years of age. Soon after he moved to the nucleus of what was to be the 8th Battalion. He applied to join the 9th Battalion where his father was Adjutant. His two brothers Alan George Frankland Bell and Haldane Frankland Bell came from respectively America and Australia to join up. So Captain Edward Henry Bell had three commissioned sons in the same Regiment.

The Ulster Division after initial training moved to Seaford in East Sussex and in October 1915 sailed for France. By this time Eric Norman Frankland Bell had become a full Lieutenant and was given charge of a Trench Mortar Battery attached to the 9th Inniskillings. It was in this capacity that he gave his life on July 1st 1916.

After the award was gazetted King George Vth wrote to Bell's father and said "It is a matter of sincere regret to me that the death of Captain E. N. F. Bell, deprived me of the pride of personally conferring on him the Victoria Cross, the greatest of all rewards for bravery and devotion to duty." The medal was given to Bell's father by the King on November 29th 1916 and is still in private hands.

Both of Bell's brothers were seriously wounded in the War but were able to return to their adopted countries. Their parents emigrated in the early 1920s to be near one of their sons.

Thiepval Memorial (D. C. Jennings)

G. S. Cather

The 36th (Ulster) Divison won four VCs on July 1st 1916 and two of them went to the 109th Bde and two to the 108th Bde. Three out of the four men were not to survive the first days of the Somme battle and Lt. Geoffrey St. George Shillington Cather of the 9th Royal Irish Fusiliers was one of them.

Although the Ulsters made great progress on the 1st towards the Schwaben Redoubt the 108th Bde on the left in its quest to capture the positions to the south-east of Beaumont Hamel and the village of Beaucourt was held up by the strong German defences. The first wave of the 9th Bn. left their trenches at 7.10 am and reached the shelter of a ravine which faced the northern side of the village of Hamel. Twenty minutes later when the battle commenced the Irish Fusiliers' first wave attempted to go forward but came under intense German machine gun fire. The following waves were mown down as they tried in their turn to reach the ravine. The 12th Irish Rifles were also met with murderous fire in their attempt to capture Beaucourt Station. Within a couple of hours the Germans had restored their positions and the battlefield was strewn with the dead and the wounded of the 108th Bde. At night after a roll call of those men who had made the attack, there were no

officer survivors and only 80 men had been left unwounded. 244 men were either killed or wounded on the 1st and this figure included nine officers. Later in the year one of the reasons for the disaster was discovered and this was that

Gallahers Cigarette Card

Hamel July 1st 1916

Cather, who was the Battalion Adjutant, went out in the evening of the 1st to help with bringing in the wounded from 'no man's land'. There was heavy German fire as he carried out this work and by midnight he had brought three men in to safety. The next day he went out again to give succour and comfort but was killed by machine gun fire at 10.30 am. He died at the age of 25 and was buried where he fell to the south of Beaumont Hamel. His grave was not found after the war and his name appears on the panels of the Thiepval Memorial, Pier and Face 15 A.

His citation which appeared in the *London Gazette* of September 8th 1916 read as follows:

"For most conspicuous bravery. From 7 p.m. till midnight he searched "No Man's Land," and brought in three wounded men.

Next morning at 8 a.m. he continued his search, brought in another wounded man, and gave water to others, arranging for their rescue later. Finally, at 10.30 a.m., he took out water to another man, and was proceeding further when he was himself killed.

one of the German machine gun positions was hidden in an emplacement on the top of a shaft which was reached by a tunnel drilled into the railway embankment on the edge of the valley of the River Ancre.

G. S. Cather   P. Hansen   D. Cather

Memorial plaque at Hazelwood School (R. W. Bawtree)

All this was carried out in full view of the enemy. and under direct machine gun fire and intermittent artillery fire.

He set a splendid example of courage and self-sacrifice."

Cather was the son of Mr R. G. Cather of Limpsfield, Surrey and Mrs Margaret Matilda Cather of 26 Priory Road, West Hampstead. He was born at Christchurch Road, Streatham Hill on October 11th 1890. He was sent to Hazelwood School, Limpsfield in September 1900 and after about three years his academic record improved before he went on to Rugby in 1905. He was never prominent at Rugby

Hazelwood School. G. S. Cather, D. Cather and P. Hansen

and had to leave when he was in the Upper Fifth as his father died in 1908 and so therefore he was unable to complete his studies. The impression that he left was of a shy, retiring and earnest young man. He joined the firm of Joseph Tetley and Co. in the City of London where his father had been a partner. In 1912 he was sent by them to America and Canada and returned in May 1914.

After war broke out in August 1914 he enlisted a few weeks later in the 19th Royal Fusiliers (2nd Public School Battalion.). His parents were both from Northern Ireland and in May 1915 he obtained a commission with the Royal Irish Fusiliers. The 9th Battalion had originally been The Armagh, Monaghan and Cavan Volunteers. He went with them as part of the 36th (Ulster) Division to France in October 1915. He became Assistant Adjutant in November and Adjutant a month later.

By the end of June 1916 his Battalion as part of the 108th Bde. attack to the north of the River Ancre was in position in front of the village of Hamel.

After his death Cather's Colonel wrote to the family as follows:

"He heard a man calling out and went over the parapet in broad daylight, gave him water, called out to see if there was anyone else within hail, saw a hand waving feebly, went on and was shot through the head by a machine gun and killed instantaneously."

"So brave and fearless: such a fine character. As an Adjutant he was perfectly wonderful, and the Battalion has sustained a severe loss by his death. . . ."

The Chaplain wrote:

. . . "He was one who lived on a very high level, and yet he was always in full sympathy with his fellow creatures, and ready at all times to extend a kindly hand.

. . . We all very much hope that his name will be added to the list of gallant heroes who have gained the V.C."

On March 31st 1917 at Buckingham Palace the King presented the medal to Cather's widowed mother and in 1979 Cather's brother Captain Dermot Cather (RN) Rtd. presented his brother's medals to the Regimental Museum in Armagh. Cather's name was commemorated at Hazelwood School on a plaque in the school chapel until the building was destroyed in the October Hurricane of 1987. The plaque has now been remounted on the wall of the main school building where the chapel used to stand. Hazelwood School also has another holder of the V.C. amongst its old boys, Captain Percy Howard Hansen.

**V. C. CATHER
G. ST G. S.**

Thiepval Memorial (D. C. Jennings)

J. L. Green

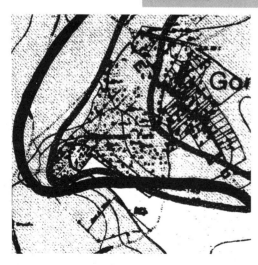

Going from right to left of the Somme battlefield Captain John Leslie Green was the last man to be awarded the VC for a deed carried out during the first 36 hours of the battle. Green was a medical officer who was attached to the 1/5th Sherwood Foresters who in turn were part of the 139th Bde of the 46th Division.

The task of the Division was to capture Gommecourt Wood on the northern side of Gommecourt village. At the same time the London Division the 56th were to take Gommecourt Park to the south. The two Divisions were then to meet up. Although this was the plan, the whole attack was in fact a diversionary attack in order to relieve enemy pressure on the battlefield further southwards. Like most British attacks on July 1st 1916 it ended in total disaster.

On the eve of the battle the 1/5th SF left

Pommier for Fonquevillers and at midnight moved up into the muddy assembly trenches. On the 1st at 6.25am they moved up to advance trenches and after throwing smoke bombs at 7.25am the battalion moved off in three waves. The fourth wave was delayed, partly because of the density of the smoke and partly because of the withering enemy machine gun fire from the wood. On the right were the 6th North Staffs Bn. and on the left were the 7th S.F. and the two battalions had great difficulty in advancing at all. Many men in the three lines of the 1/5th SF reached the second line but as the first line had not been cleared it meant that the troops could be shot from behind as well as from the front. Captain Green advanced in the rear of his battalion and on reaching the German wire found a brother officer lying seriously wounded.

The officer's name was Captain Robinson and he was the 139th Bde machine gun officer. His task was to be responsible for two machine gun sections of the 1/5th SF attached to the 139th Machine Gun Company. The machine gunners were wiped out before covering more than 150 yards and Robinson had gone on and reached the enemy wire where he was wounded and became entangled on the enemy wire. Green moved Robinson when they were both under very heavy fire and dragged him into a shell hole where he dressed his wounds. He then carried him back to the British positions and on reaching the advanced trench Robinson was hit again. Once more Green dressed his wounds when he himself was shot in the head and killed. Robinson was eventually brought in but was to die two days later. The 1/5th SF

Fonquevillers July 1st 1916

were relieved at 6.10pm after a day of disaster, their casualties being 491 out of the 734 men that they began the day with. They remained in the Bellacourt area for the rest of July.

———————

Gallahers Cigarette Card

John Leslie Green was born in a house called Coneygarths which is in the High Street at Buckden in the former county of Huntingdonshire. This is now part of Cambridgeshire. He was the son of Mr John George Green and Florence May Green. John George was a local landowner and Justice of the Peace. St. Marys Church, Buckden contains the tombs of many of the Green family. John Leslie Junior was Baptised in Buckden Church on January 12th 1889 and was known as

Leslie in order to distinguish him from his father. Leslie went to school at Felsted School (1902-1906) in north Essex and then went up to Cambridge where he studied at Downing College. He obtained Honours in Part l of the Natural Sciences Tripos in 1910. He was also a keen rower and an all round sportsman. He rowed for his college. He trained for a career in medicine at St Bartholomews Hospital London and became House Surgeon at Huntingdon County Hospital. He became medically qualified in 1913 and on the outbreak of War in 1914 was given a commission in the Royal Army Medical Corps. He was at first attached to the 5th South Staffs and then the Field Ambulance, before transferring to the Sherwood Foresters. On January lst 1916 he married Miss Edith Mary Nesbitt Moss a fellow Doctor. She was the daughter of Mr F. J. Moss of Stainfield Hall, Lincolnshire.

Fonquevillers Military Cemetery (D. C. Jennings)

Fonquevillers Military Cemetery (C.W.G.C.)

The chief witness of Green's heroism was Captain Frank Bradbury Robinson (6th S.F.) before he died of his wounds on July 3rd. He is buried at Warlincourt Halte British Cemetery in Plot 1, Row F. Grave 6. The citation for Green's V.C. was published only five weeks later in the *London Gazette* of August 5th and read:

"For most conspicuous devotion to duty. Although himself wounded, he went to the assistance of an officer who had been wounded and was hung up on the enemy's wire entanglements, and succeeded in dragging him to a shell hole, where he dressed his wounds, notwithstanding that bombs and rifle grenades were thrown at him the whole time.

Captain Green then endeavoured to bring the wounded officer into safe cover, and had nearly succeeded in doing so when he was himself killed."

The General commanding 139th Bde wrote to Green's widow:

"Dear Mrs Green, I have seen the letter you wrote to the Officer Commanding the 5th Sherwood Foresters, asking for news of your husband. I am deeply grieved to have to tell you that I am afraid that there is no doubt that your husband was killed on 1st July, and that I should like to say how much I feel for you in your sorrow, but at the same time I must express my intense admiration for the manner in which he met his death. . . . . ."

Green was 27 when he was killed and his body was buried in Fonquevillers Cemetery Plot lll, Row D Grave 15. His widow who had been on the staff of Nottingham Hospital collected the V.C. from the hands of the King on October 7th. She later remarried and presented her first husband's medals to the R.A.M.C.

Green had a sister and a younger brother Sec. Lt. Edward Alan Green who was with the 1/5th South Staffs. He was killed on October 2nd 1915 and has no known grave.

Coneygarths (W. Fullaway)

In 1920 Green's father wrote to the Buckden Parish Council and suggested that he would freely donate a memorial to the men of the village who had been killed in the war. For some reason this offer was rejected and Green went ahead anyway and on land that he owned next to Coneygarths, the family home, he erected a memorial stone to his two sons and also the dead of the village in 1921. However only the two names are listed. This memorial fell into decay but was later 'rediscovered' and repaired in time for a service of rededication on July lst 1986, the 70th anniversary of the Battle of the Somme and of Green's death. Opposite the memorial stone and birthplace of Green is Buckden Towers, a former home for the use of the Bishops of Lincoln. In the Great War it was used as a Military Hospital. St Mary's Church where Green was christened has a memorial to the village of both wars and so the Green brothers are commemorated twice in the village. Leslie is also listed on the memorial at Downing College Cambridge.

Felsted School has two former pupils who gained the V.C., one from the Afghan War and Leslie Green from the First War. There was a plaque to their memory in the school chapel. The chapel was modernised in the 1960s and the plaque along with part of the wooden school war memorial was lost. In the mid 1980s it was felt that the two Felsted VCs should once more be remembered and funds were collected and a new plaque to

Memorial to Green Brothers, Buckden (W. Fullaway)

both men was rededicated on Remembrance Sunday in 1986. The school (1990) is planning a trip to the Somme Battlefields that will take place in 1991 and no doubt they will be visiting the grave of one of their most famous old boys. One other reminder of Green is the former Huntingdon County Hospital Building which has changed its use but still stands on the outskirts of the town. His medals are in the possession of the R.A.M.C.

LIEUT W·R·P HAMILTON
Queen Victoria's Own Corps of Guides
FUTTEHABAD · SECOND AFGHAN WAR
1879

CAPT J·L GREEN
Royal Army Medical Corps
THE SOMME · FIRST WORLD WAR
1916

Felsted School (W. Fullaway)

S. W. Loudoun-Shand

The 10th Green Howards were in the 62nd Bde of the 21st Division whose objective on July lst 1916 was the village of Fricourt. Two days before they had been in billets in Buire and on the night of the 30th June they were positioned in front of the wood south of Bécourt Wood called Queen's Redoubt.

On the lst the battalion were in support to the main attack and it was at this time that the Green Howards gained the first of what were to be four V.C.s for the battle of the Somme. Tempory Major S. W. Loudoun-Shand's citation in the *London Gazette* of September 8th read as follows:

"For most conspicuous bravery. When his company attempted to climb over the parapet to attack the enemy's trenches they were met by very fierce machine-gun fire which temporarily stopped their progress. Major Loudoun-Shand immediately leapt on the parapet, helped the men over it and encouraged them in every way until he fell mortally wounded. Even then he insisted on being propped up in the trench, and went on encouraging the non-commissioned officers and men until he died."

The battalion was relieved by the 10th Lancashire Fusiliers in Shelter Wood in the early evening. Shand's body was brought back and buried in Norfolk Cemetery (I.C.77).

In an article that appeared in *The Legion* former Corporal Harry Fellows of the 12th Northumberland Fusiliers had this to say of Shand's action.

"the Green Howards led the attack north of Fricourt, with my own battalion in support, some 400 yards to the rear. When the barrage lifted, the German machine gunners had scrambled from their dugouts, manned the guns and swept a murderous hail of fire across No Man's Land. With such a savage fire overhead the Green Howards had shown

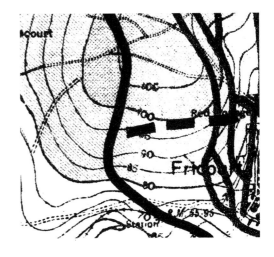

Fricourt July 1st 1916

Gallahers Cigarette Card

a reluctance to leave the trench. But the Major had mounted the parapet and urged his men over the top.

Had the Green Howards faltered we should certainly have been called into action to advance over the open ground. It was then that we Northumberlands realised the great debt we owed to that one gallant officer. Since that day he has remained my hero of the Great War."

Fellows visited the Norfolk Cemetery in 1984 the first time back and paid tribute to Shand by laying a wreath at his grave.

S. W. Loudoun-Shand (IWM)

Norfolk Cemetery (C.W.G.C.)

Stewart Loudoun-Shand was born in Ceylon on October 8th 1879. He was the second son of Mr and Mrs J. Loudoun-Shand who had five sons and five daughters. The family fortune was made from tea. The family moved to Dulwich in South London and lived at Craigelie, Alleyn Park. The boys went to Dulwich College and Stewart was a distinguished Athlete and Cricketer. His youngest brother E. G. Shand was later to play for Oxford University Rugger Team and later played for Scotland. Stewart left College early and took up an appointment with William Deacon's Bank. When the South African War broke out Stewart enlisted with the London Scottish but was considered too young for active service. He then managed to

Norfolk Cemetery (D. C. Jennings)

switch to the Pembroke Yeomanry and served with them throughout the war. He then accepted a post in Port Elizabeth with a mercantile company and stayed three years before returning to a position in Ceylon which his father had procured for him. When war broke out in 1914 Shand hurried home to England to volunteer and was given a commission with the 10th Green Howards, a Service Battalion. His rank was that of Lieutenant. He was promoted to Captain on June 14th 1915 and became Major on December 12th 1915. The battalion was involved in the Battle of Loos in September 1915 with the result of very heavy casualties which resulted in rapid promotion for Shand, his Colonel and two Majors having been killed. The orders for the Battalion for July lst 1916 were to attack to the north of Fricourt as part of a planned encircling movement.

Although his medals have been shown in public they are still kept by the family but the Green Howards Museum is fortunate enough to own the medals of their other three Somme V.C. holders.

Dulwich College War Memorial (G. Gliddon)

W. F. McFadzean

At just before 7.00am on July lst Billy McFadzean gave his life in saving his friends, which was to result in the award of a posthumous Victoria Cross. As members of the 14th Royal Irish Rifles (109th Bde.) and of the 36th (Ulster) Division they were in Thiepval Wood getting ready to advance half an hour later. The barrage was at its height and the Germans were seeking out the Ulster Division's positions with their heavy shelling. McFadzean was involved with the distribution of bombs and picked up a box of grenades and cut the cord around it. The next moment the box slipped and

W. F. McFadzean (IWM)

two bombs fell out, shedding their pins as they did so. McFadzean knew that there would be an explosion in four seconds and threw himself down on the bottom of the trench and smothered the blast from the two bombs. He was instantaneously killed and he had saved the lives of his comrades, although two were injured by the blast and Private George Gillespie, who was on McFadzean's left had to have a leg amputated. Some accounts say that he was blown to pieces and when his remains were later carried away on a stretcher the men removed their helmets in salute to their brave colleague. Many openly wept.

Near Thiepval Wood July 1st 1916

His citation which was published in the *London Gazette* of September 9th read as follows:

"For most conspicuous bravery. While in a concentration trench and opening a box of bombs for distribution prior to an attack, the box slipped down into the trench, which was crowded with men, and two of the safety pins fell out. Private McFadzean, instantly realising the danger to his comrades, threw himself on the top of the bombs.

The bombs exploded blowing him to pieces but only one other man was injured. He well knew the danger, being himself a bomber, but without a moment's hesitation he gave his life for his colleagues."

McFadzean's body was never found and he is commemorated on the Thiepval Memorial (Pier and Face 15A and 15B)

His was the first of fifty one V.C.s to be awarded during the Somme campaign.

William Frederick McFadzean was born at Lurgan Co. Armagh on October 9th 1895. He was the eldest son of William McFadzean and Mrs McFadzean of Rubicon, Cregagh, Belfast. The family lived at Cregagh which is a suburb of Belfast. McFadzean was always known as Billy and he went to school at Mountpottinger National School, and the Trade Preparatory School of the Municipal Technical Intstitute.

On completing his education he was apprenticed to the linen manufacturer, Spence, Bryson & Co., of Great Victoria Street Belfast. Billy was a very keen junior rugby player for the Collegians' Rugby Football Club. Being six foot in height and weighing thirteen stone, he was ideally suited for the game.

He joined the 1st Battalion Ballynafeigh and Newtownbreda, East Belfast Regiment. On September 22nd 1914 he joined the 14th Btn. Royal Irish Rifles

Thiepval Memorial (C.W.G.C.)

(Young Citizens) as a Private. This was in response to the call to the Volunteers to join a division which was to be the 36th (Ulster) Division. His Battalion trained at Finner Camp, Prandalstown before going to England for further training at Seaford and Liphook. The Division sailed for France in October 1915.

After Billy's death on July lst 1916 his father who was a Belfast JP received many letters including one from the CO of the 14th Royal Irish Rifles Lt. Col. F. C. Bowen:

"It was with feelings of deep pride that I read the announcement of the granting of the V.C. to your gallant son, and my only regret is that he was not spared to us to wear his well-earned decoration. It was one of the very finest deeds of a war that is so full of big things, and I can assure you that the whole battalion rejoiced when they heard it. . ."

Lt. Col R. D. Spencer Chichester who raised the 14th RIR also wrote:

"I was greatly grieved to hear of his death at the time that I heard of his magnificent and heroic deed. I did not write you then as I knew he was recommended for the Victoria Cross, and I waited to do so till it should have been definitely conferred on him. . ."

The King also wrote, on December 18th 1916 and William McFadzean senior was given a third class ticket with which to travel to London and collect his son's medal. The ceremony took place on February 28th 1917 at Buckingham Palace and the King said: "I have very great pleasure in presenting to you the Victoria Cross for your son, the late Private McFadzean. I deeply regret that he did not live to receive it personally, but I am sure you are proud of your son; nothing finer has been done in this war for which I have yet given the Victoria Cross, than the act performed by your son in giving his life so heroically to save the lives of his comrades."

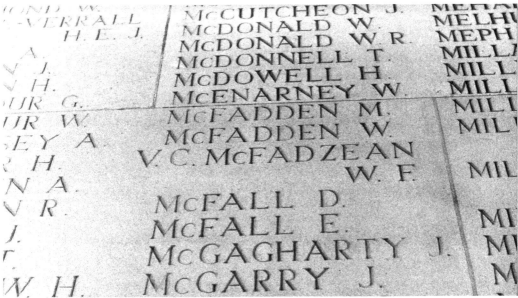

Thiepval Memorial (D. C. Jennings)

A year after Billy's death a service was held at his church at Newtownbreda Presbyterian Church on the outskirts of Belfast in order to commemorate his life. A plaque was also unveiled by Col. Barlow D.S.O. General Staff Officer, Northern District Irish Command. The church service was taken by Rev. Dr Workman who quoted these words from St John's Gospel "Greater love hath no man than this that a man lay down his life for his friends."

Billy was said to be a very popular soldier and one to keep up the spirit of cheerfulness and apparently his favourite song was "My Little Grey Home in the West" which he was said to have been singing shortly before his death.

His Victoria Cross Medal is usually kept in a bank vault but in 1989 his nephew, also a William took it to France with him when on a short trip to the battlefields.

William McFadzean July 1989 (Belfast Tel.)

R. Quigg

Gallahers Cigarette Card

The fourth man of the 36th (Ulster) Division to win the Victoria Cross and the only one of the four who lived to wear it was Robert Quigg. Like Cather and McFadzean he was involved with saving life rather than with killing the enemy. He was a member of the 12th Royal Irish Rifles who on July 1st 1916 were

Hamel July 1st 1916

assembled in front line trenches to the north west of the village of Hamel. His Battalion was part of the 108th Bde.

On the eve of July 1st his platoon commander Sir Harry Macnaghten was reported missing, and Private Quigg went out into 'no man's land' no fewer than seven times to try and find him. Instead of bringing in Sir Harry he brought in seven other men and saved their lives. Sir Harry's body was never found.

His citation for the V.C. was published in the *London Gazette* of September 9th and it was as follows:

"For most conspicuous bravery. He advanced to the assault with his platoon three times. Early next morning, hearing a rumour that his platoon officer was lying out wounded, he went out seven times to look for him under heavy shell and machine gun fire, each time bringing back a wounded man. The last man he dragged in on a waterproof sheet from within a few yards of the enemy's wire.

He was seven hours engaged in this most gallant work, and finally was so exhausted that he had to give it up."

Robert Quigg was born on February 28th 1885 at Cornkirk, Giants Causeway, Northern Ireland. His father, whose name was also Robert was a boatman and tourist guide on the Causeway. Robert junior attended the Giants Causeway National School. He became a farm labourer and worked on the Macnaghten Estate. Sir Harry whose life Robert was to try and save on July 1st 1916 was born in 1896. In September 1914 Quigg joined the Royal Irish Rifles (Central Antrim) as

Memorial to Sir Harry Macnaghten (Bushmills or nearby)

a Private and Macnaghten joined as a Second Lieutenant. They left for England with the rest of the 36th (Ulster) Division in October 1915 and unlike most recipients of the V.C. Quigg did not go to Buckingham Palace but to York Cottage,

A galaxy of Ulster heroes 1954, Quigg second from the left (Belfast Tel.)

Sandringham, Norfolk, on January 8th 1917. It was reported that the King after congratulating him asked Quigg whether he was married and received the reply: -

"No Sir, but after what has happened to me I supppose I soon will be." This rejoinder very much amused the King who Quigg was later to have described "as a brave wee man". On his return to Bushmills, his parish, he was given a great reception for not only trying to save the life of the local squire but also of course for winning what was to be one of the four Somme VCs for the Ulster Division. At a reception at Hamill Hotel, Bushmills, Quigg was presented with £200 in Exchequer Bonds. Sir Harry's mother Lady Macnaghten presented him with a gold watch as a mark of appreciation. Later when he was hard up he was to sell this watch for £100.

After 1916 Quigg served in Mesopotamia and Egypt and reached the rank of Sergeant. He served in the whole of the European War and later was declared as not reaching Army Physical Requirements. He had had an accident in 1926 which left him partly paralysed and finally left the Army in 1926. After the war his figure was used as a model for the local war memorial and he spent the rest of his life in a cottage on the Macnaghten estate. He never married.

In 1953 Queen Elizabeth II visited Ulster and Quigg was presented to her. In May 1954 at Ulster Hall he was one of five Northern Irishmen who had all won the VC to be presented with a silver tankard. A picture of this group taken by a local newspaper tells us more about what sort of man Quigg was than a hundred words does! He died at the age of 70 at Dalriada Hospital, Ballycastle, on May 14th 1955. He was buried at Billy Parish Church, Bushmills. At his funeral there was an escort party of fifty men from the Royal

Billy Parish Churchyard, Bushmills

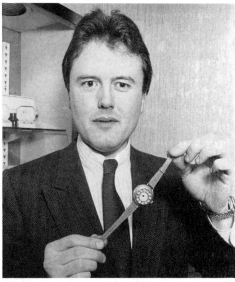

Harold Brown with Quigg's watch 1988 (D. C. Thomson)

Ulster Rifles Depot. His oak coffin was draped with the Union Jack and his medals were carried separately. A bugler played *The Last Post* and *Reveille*.

In 1958 at the instigation of the Royal British Legion a simple granite headstone was placed on Quigg's grave and unveiled by the Lord Lieutenant of County Antrim, Lord Rathcavan on November 16th. There was a large attendance of the Royal Ulster Rifles and of former comrades. At his death Quigg was survived by a brother and four sisters. His watch given him by Lady Macnaghten turned up at a house clearance in 1988. His medals which number eight or nine include the Medal of the Order of St. George of Russia and the Croix de Guerre. They are in the hands of the Regimental Museum in Belfast.

W. Ritchie

On the extreme left of the positions of the 36th (Ulster) Division was the right flank of the 29th Division whose task was to capture the Y Ravine and the southern section of the village of Beaumont Hamel. On their left was the 4th Division whose task was to capture the ground to the north of this village which included the Redan positions.

Drummer Ritchie was a member of the 2nd Seaforth Highlanders of the 10th Bde of the 4th Division. The other two Brigades in the Division were the 11th and the 12th. The 11th Bde. was to go forward with its immediate objective being the last trench in the German Front Line System which was called Munich Trench. The 10th and the 12th Bdes.

Gallahers Cigarette Card

were to move forward slightly later after having given the 11th time to capture their objective. The two following Bdes. were to go through the lines of the 11th. That

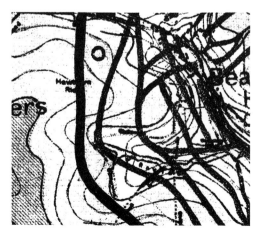

was the plan.

For two hours before 7.30am intense British artillery fire was concentrated on the German positions. At zero hour the 11th Bde moved off in waves. An hour and a quarter later no message had been received by the following Bdes and they moved off including the 2nd Seaforth Highlanders. There was very heavy machine gun fire from the Germans and it was obvious that the 11th Bde had not reached its objective and further more had been ruthlessly cut down. Communi-

Beaumont Hamel July 1st 1916

cation was almost non existent and in mid morning when the 3rd line was being evacuated, men of various units were drifting back to the Allied positions. Officer casualties were very high and the men were virtually leaderless. Drummer Ritchie had disobeyed the standard instruction about leaving musical instruments behind before an attack and clambered onto the top of a German trench and repeatedly sounded the

"Charge" with the idea of stemming the drift back of the British troops to their own trenches. This action together with his conduct throughout the day was to gain him the Victoria Cross. The necessary eyewitnesses of Ritchie's bravery were Captain J. Laurie and Lt. Col. J. O. Hopkinson who were the Adjutant and the Officer Commanding. At the end of the day these two officers, two wounded officers and about eighty other ranks were all the men left from the Seaforths. They had been relieved at about 2am on July 2nd. They returned to bivouacs in some gorse behind the village of Mailly-Maillet. Next day they were inspected by the Corps Commander Lt. Gen Sir Aylmer Hunter Weston.

Ritchie's citation was published in the *London Gazette* of September 9th:

"For most conspicuous bravery and resource, when on his own initiative he stood on the parapet of an enemy trench, and under heavy machine gun fire and bomb attacks, repeatedly sounded the "Charge", thereby rallying many men of various units, who, having lost their units, were wavering and beginning to retire.

This action showed the highest type of courage and personal initiative.

Throughout the day Drummer Ritchie carried messages over fire-swept ground, showing the greatest devotion to duty."

Later he commented "that if things had gone the other way he would have been court-martialled and not decorated." He received the V.C. from the hands of the King on November 25th 1916.

———

Walter Potter Ritchie was born at 81 Hopefield Road, Glasgow on March 27th 1892. His father's name was also Walter and his mother's maiden name was Helen Monteith Murphy. After leaving school he was apprenticed briefly to a blacksmith and was an ardent member of the Episcopal Church at Troon in Glasgow. He joined the 8th Scottish Rifles when under age and in August 1908 at the age of 16 transferred to the 2nd Seaforth Highlanders as a Drummer. He was a member of the original British Expeditionary Force and took part in the Battle of Mons and was wounded in October 1914 in a village just outside Armentieres. Later in the war the battalion moved down to the Somme sector and spent a lot of time in the village of Mailly Maillet before the 'Big Push'. After being given the V.C. in November 1916 Ritchie returned to Glasgow, arriving at St Enoch Station at 8pm on November 26th or 27th. He was met by a group of friends but did not want to expand on information about his exploit. "If you were to drop a Jack Johnson at ma feet ", he observed, "you couldna' mak' me speak."

He was wounded in 1917 and before the war was to end he was gassed twice and wounded twice more. He always carried his bugle although Buglers had ceased to be employed as such early in the war. After the war he joined the 1st Seaforths at Belfast in July 1921 when he was promoted to the rank of Sergeant, and appointed Drum-Major of the Btn. He held this position until he left the Army in 1929. He later became a Recruiting Officer in Glasgow. He died at West Saville Terrace, Mayfield in Edinburgh on March 17th 1965 at the age of 72. He was cremated three days later at the Warriston Crematorium. The bugle that he sounded the "Charge" with is now at the Queens Own Highlanders Museum, Fort George in Inverness. In 1970 his medals came up for sale at Sothebys and were sold for £1700. Eleven years later they came up for sale again, this time in Australia and are in private hands.

W. P. Ritchie

G. Sanders

The l/7th West Yorkshire Battalion was part of the 146th Bde of the 49th Division. At the beginning of the Battle of the Somme the role of the Division was to provide support to the 36th (Ulster) Division and the 32nd Division. The Headquarters of the l/7th West Yorks together with its sister battalion the l/8th West Yorks was at Belfast City in Aveluy Wood. They were due east of the Leipzig Salient which was to be the only position on the north side of the River Ancre where the British were going to hold ground captured, on the first day of the battle.

During the battle on July 1st the l/7th was one of the battalions that was ordered up to help the 32nd Division. Their role was to help with the capture of the strongly held German position, the Schwaben Redoubt. At around 8. 30 p.m. a company of the l/7th and l/8th

West Yorks. battalions provided a defensive flank that faced north at the Schwaben Redoubt in order to assist the 107th Bde already there. There was confusion and when darkness fell the two West Yorks companies withdrew. There were many casualties amongst the officers and the other ranks.

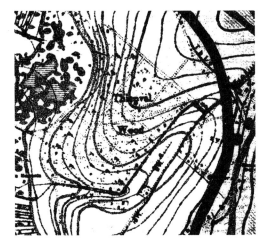

Gallahers Cigarette Card

However a company under the leadership of Corporal G. Sanders decided to continue the fight with the enemy in German trenches close to Thiepval. The German stronghold village was to the south of Schwaben Redoubt. Corporal Sanders was to win the V.C. for what happened next and his citation was published in the *London Gazette* of September 9th as follows:

"For most conspicuous bravery. After an advance into the enemy's trenches, he found himself isolated with a party of thirty men. He organised his defences, and impressed on his men that his and their duty was to hold the position at all costs.

Next morning he drove off an attack by the enemy and rescued some prisoners who had fallen into their hands. Later two strong bombing attacks were beaten off. On the following day he was relieved after showing the greatest courage, determination and good leadership during 36 hours of very trying conditions.

All this time his party was without food and water, having given all their water to the wounded during the first night. After the relieving force was firmly established, he brought his party, nineteen strong, back to our trenches."

At this time Thiepval and Aveluy Woods had become an absolute nightmare of war. Many of the frontline trenches had been smashed by the German artillery and the wounded were clustered together for support. There was total confusion.

———

Near Thiepval July 1st 1916

George Sanders was the son of Thomas Sanders and Amy Sanders of 3 Shand Grove, Holbeck, Leeds. He was born at New Wortley, Leeds on July 8th 1894. He was the youngest in a family of seven and was educated at Little Holbeck School and became a choirboy at St. Johns Church. His mother died when he was nine years old. When he left school he became a fitter's apprentice at the Airedale Foundry. On November 9th 1914 he enlisted with the Leeds Rifles which became the l/7th West Yorkshire Battalion. In April 1915 his unit which had become part of the 146th Bde. left for France and were soon in Flanders, in the Ypres Salient. They lost heavily in a gas attack in the line to the south of Boesinge. In the spring of 1916 they were transferred to the Somme region for the 'Big Push'. and arrived on the west side of the River Ancre on June 30th and marched to take up their positions in Aveluy Wood to the north of the main track through the wood which led to Martinsart, a village behind the wood.

When Sanders' award of the V.C. was announced in September 1916 he became the third Leeds man to gain this distinction and the first Leeds Territorial to win it. On November 14th he returned to Leeds for the first time since his award was announced and by this time he had been promoted from Corporal to Sergeant. His family were only warned of his arrival the day before and there was little time to organise a welcoming ceremony. Nevertheless a large crowd turned out to greet the 'local hero' at the Midland Station platform and they included his family and his former colleagues at the Airedale Foundry. Sanders wore the ribbon of the VC on his breast and had a wound stripe on his arm. He was given three cheers and when he emerged into the City Square the crowd was even more numerous. He was taken to the Town Hall and greeted by the Lord Mayor. He was, according to the *Yorkshire Evening Post* "Like most other heroes, not too willing to refer to the deed which won him fame, but he did mention that out of the 32 men who went into the trench only 19 came out of it." . . . "Five of them got Military Medals, however, and unfortunately one, Cpl Kirk, has since been killed."

Although he was seemingly unaware of when he was to be given his V.C. on the 14th he actually must have travelled to London the next day to receive his award at Buckingham Palace. It emerged that he was recommended by the Commanding Officer of the Royal Irish Rifles whom Sanders' men were supporting and not by his own Commanding Officer Lt. Col. A. E. Kirk who nevertheless was delighted when he heard the news of the award. He wrote as follows: "They went up gallantly and suffered heavy losses. All the officers out of Sanders' platoon had gone, and he took command of the platoon and held on and organised a fine resistance."

A few days later Sanders was back in Leeds again for a more formal reception from the City Council than before. This time he was greeted and thanked in public by the Lord Mayor on the steps of the Town Hall. There was again a large crowd and this time enhanced by a Guard of Honour. The Council was keen to award Sanders with a gift or donation but at this time the War Office had forbidden soldiers from receiving gifts of money. The Council were therefore going to think up an alternative.

Sanders was given a commission on June 27th 1917 and gazetted to the 2nd Prince of Wales' Own (West Yorkshire Regiment (attached to the l/6th Bn. He was made Acting Captain on December 15th later in the year. By April his battalion were back in the Ypres sector and he became a prominent figure in the fighting during the German attack of April 1918 and was taken prisoner at Kemmel Hill on April 25th. He was posted as wounded and missing. In his absence he was awarded the MC. He was last seen wounded in the leg and right arm, but carrying his revolver in his left hand. Three months later however his family heard from him at Limburg where he had been taken as a prisoner of war. He was repatriated on Boxing Day 1918. and demobilized on March 20th the following year.

After the war he worked on the staff of the Meadow Lane gas-works which was then under Leeds Corporation and later taken over by the North-Eastern Gas Board. In the Second War he was the

G. Sanders

Officer Commanding of the Home Guard at the Gas Works. He died at the age of 55 at St James Hospital, Leeds, after a long illness on April 4th 1950. His home was at Stratford Street, Dewsbury Road.

He was given a full military funeral and four other VC holders attended. Three volleys were fired as the coffin left the chapel and two Regimental Buglers sounded the *Last Post* and *Reveille*. The coffin was draped with the Union Jack and Sanders' medals were carried by his former Sgt. Major. Mr Frank Stembridge. Apart from his family those who attended were the Leeds Rifles Old Comrades Association, the Home Guard, the British Legion, and the Leeds

Group of the North-East Gas Board. The firing party had been chosen from the 45th Btn. Royal Tank Regt (TA) who were successors of the 7th (Leeds Rifles) Battalion, West Yorkshire Regiment. After the funeral on April 6th Sanders' body was cremated at the Cottingley Crematorium.

His widow Nellie Sanders kept her husband's medals which are in private hands. Sanders was commemorated in the New Leeds Rifles (TA) Museum at Carlton Old Barracks Leeds. In 1937 there had been a plan to commemorate the Leeds V.C.s but it had come to nothing.

Four V.C.s at Thiepval hero's funeral

Four V.C.s at Thiepval hero's funeral (YEN   April 6th 1950)

J. Y. Turnbull

James Turnbull, a master joiner married Elizabeth Dunlop at Dunoon on December 29th 1870 and they were to have three sons all of whom were to have a role to play in the Great War. James Senior was well known in Glasgow business circles and James junior was born on Christmas Eve 1883, the family name of Yuill was given to him as a middle name. James Yuill was educated at Albert Road Academy, Glasgow and on leaving School he was employed for a time by Wallace Scott and Co. a firm of wholesale speciality tailors. He later transferred to Messrs Wm. Chalmers of Oban. He had grown up a very tall man who towered above the average man and was always known as "Jimmy". He was a keen amateur footballer and trained with the Glasgow Third Lanark Volunteers.

At the outbreak of war he joined one of the Glasgow Battalions which in turn became the 17th Highland Light Infantry Battalion and because of his pre-war training he rose in rank rapidly to that of Sergeant. He had a brother named Gavin who served with the Royal Engineers and another who was attached to the Canadian pay department in London.

On the eve of the Somme battle Turnbull had been a Sergeant for seven or eight months. His battalion the 17th H.L.I. were part of the 97th Bde of the 32nd Division. They had spent the night before the day of the battle in huts in Bouzincourt and had to jouney to the front line via trenches between Aveluy and Authuille. The line in which they had had to spend the night of June 30th had been virtually blown out of existence and

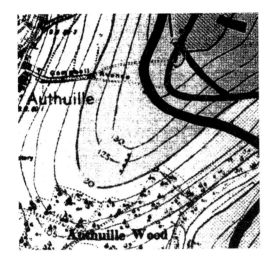

they took up their battle positions at 6.25am on the lst. Their aim was to take and hold a position called the Leipzig Salient which was part of the German front line. The task was an impossible one as the Germans overlooked the Allied advance from three sides.

We are fortunate in having an eyewitness account of what happened to Turnbull which first appeared as an interview with a colleague of his Lance-Corporal McKechnie. It was printed in *The Glasgow Herald* of November 28th 1916.

"It was during a recent attack that Turnbull performed his brave deed. He was one of the first to go over the parapet, and I was near him all the time, an eye witness of what he did. We took the first line of German trenches fairly easily and when we were passing through there, Turnbull who was always on the alert, noticed a large German bomb store which had been abandoned. He indicated the store as we passed on and shouted out that in the event of our running short of bombs he would send some of the men back to the place. He was a fellow who always took charge of affairs, but we all

Leipzig Salient July 1st 1916

Sergt. J. Y. TURNBULL, V.C.
Photo : Central News

Gallahers Cigarette Card

were threatening to outflank us and this would have meant the cutting off of the complete battalion, Sergeant Turnbull however saved the situation by his initiative. He kept men carrying bombs to him, and he continued the bombing on his own until our own supply ran short. Then his foreknowledge of the German bomb store behind proved of value. Men were sent back to bring in bombs from this place. Occasionally if he ran short of bombs, and the men had not returned in time, he seized hold of a machine-gun and played it on the Germans. He kept this up for about sixteen hours, practically holding up the whole of the German flank and saving the battalion. Our position was held in this way until the battalion was relieved, and it was practically all due to Turnbull's courage and

had the greatest confidence in his judgement. We got held up at the second line trenches, which were flanked on either side by redoubts. Turnbull's party, of which I was a member were told to attack the redoubt which was on our left flank. We met with considerable opposition. Turnbull had a splendid physique and was almost fearless. He was a fine cricketer, and it was possibly this that made him such an expert bomber. He could throw a bomb further than any other man in the battalion. At the beginning the fighting was pretty fierce, and we had to 'carry on' for about fourteen hours. Most of the men were exhausted by that time. The Germans

J. Y. Turnbull

tenacity. His stamina was really remarkable, as most of the others were quite fagged out with what they had gone through. He was killed not long after that, during a momentary lull. With his usual activity he had been hustling around to see what was happening, and when he was crossing from the redoubt to behind a second line trench, a sniper got him."

The Regimental History tells a similar story: "At 7.30am the 17th H.L.I. on the right and the 16th H.L.I. on the left crept out of their trenches and moved close up to the German wire under cover of the barrage. This was by order of the Bde. Commander Brigadier-General J. B. Jardine, as an alternative to the usual practice at that time of advancing in extended waves. The 17th H. L. I. had no luck this day. When they rose up they immediately came under heavy enfilade fire from the ruins of Thiepval; the wire was intact but for the occasional gaps which were covered." . . . "They had with them sappers, carrying Bangalore torpedoes, for it had been realised that the

Lonsdale Cemetery (D. C. Jennings)

barrage had not been effective on the wire in this sector, but they were all shot down on the wire." . . . "The 17th H.L.I. pushed on towards the second line, but the failure on their left exposed their flank and the leading companies were all shot down. The remainder consolidated the first line—the Leipzig Redoubt and held it. Their casualties were 22 officers and 447 other ranks. They gained a Victoria Cross, posthumous: Sergeant James Yuill Turnbull."

Turnbull was described as 'being very popular with the men' and as 'a strong forthright personality.' Lt. A. N. Drysdale in a letter to Turnbull's father paid a tribute to his abilities as a platoon sergeant, and referred to the deep regret felt by the whole battalion."

Turnbull was buried at the Lonsdale Cemetery, Authuille (IV. G.9) His award was gazetted on September 25th.

"For most conspicuous bravery and devotion to duty, when, having with his party captured a post apparently of great importance to the enemy, he was subjected to severe counter-attacks, which were continuous throughout the whole day. Although his party was wiped out and replaced several times during the day. Sergeant Turnbull never wavered in his determination to hold the post, the loss of which would have been very serious. Almost single-handed, he maintained his position, and displayed the highest degree of valour and skill in the performance of his duties.

Later in the day this very gallant soldier was killed whilst bombing a counter-attack from the parados of our trench."

The V.C. was presented to Turnbull's father and sister at Buckingham Palace on May 2nd 1917. The whereabouts of the medal is unknown but must be in private hands.

The late Lt. G. St. G. S. CATHER
9th Royal Irish Fusiliers.

The late Pte. W. F. Mc FADZEAN
14th Royal Irish Rifles.

The late Capt. E. N. F. BELL
9th Royal Inniskilling Fusiliers.

• Pte. R. QUIGG •
12th Royal Irish Rifles.

The Late 2/Lt. J. S. EMERSON
9th Royal Inniskilling Fusiliers.

V.C.s of the Ulster Division

A. Carton de Wiart

La Boisselle was a very strongly held German position to the north east of Albert and to the south of the main Albert-Bapaume Road. Any troops attacking it from the direction of Becourt would have to advance along Sausage Valley through "no man's land" and into the German trench system to the south-east of the village. Despite the blowing of a huge mine at Lochnagar just before the battle began, on the 1st of July, as well as the previous seven days of Allied bombardment, the 34th Division was ruthlessly cut down in its attempts to capture the village. The enemy had not been visible to the naked eye as he had been cleverly concealed underground in strong dugouts.

After the retirement of the 34th Division, when it had been two days in the front line, the Division which had been in its support, the 19th, were given the task of capturing La Boisselle. The 19th (Western) Division consisted of three brigades; the 56th, 57th and 58th. The 8th Gloster Battalion were part of the 57th Bde and their commanding officer was Adrian Carton de Wiart who already had the reputation of being a very courageous soldier and was about to add to his reputation by winning a Victoria Cross.

At the start of the battle the 8th Glosters had moved from the village of Millencourt to the Intermediate Line to the north of Albert. Later on, on the 1st of July they moved up to a valley close to the Albert-Pozieres Road. At 10pm they moved again, to the trenches in the Tara-Usna Line and remained there for the night, and all through the next day. At 1.30 am on the 3rd, the battalion moved forward to attack via St Andrews Trench.

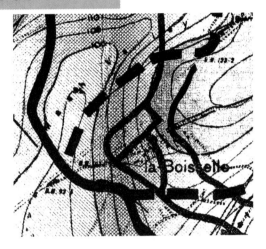

At 3.15 am they attacked La Boisselle and consolidated their positions. They remained there all day and night and in the bitter fighting had six officers killed. The other Battalions in the 57th Bde involved in the heavy fighting for the capture of the village had been the 10th Worcs, 8th N. Staffs and the 10th R. Warwicks. The Bde. had attacked from the north of the

Pre Great War

village, whilst their sister Bde. the 58th had attacked from the south.

At 11 a.m. the Germans, who had been considerably reinforced, attacked the 57th Bde., and the North Staffs, the Worcesters and the Glosters were forced back to a line about half way through the village. At around 12.30 p.m. the situation for the British was absolutely critical but the 57th Bde. were strong enough to hold the position which was marked by a hedge. It was felt that if the line had given way that the village would undoubtedly have been lost. That the line did hold was due in large measure to the gallantry of Lt. Col. A. Carton de Wiart. He was not only the commanding officer of the 8th Glosters but as the commanders of the 8th N. Staffs and of the 10th Worcesters had been killed and the commanding officer of the 10th Warwicks

wounded he had now become responsible for the 57th Bde. Carton de Wiart took a very active part in the fighting and this included drawing the pins out of grenades with his teeth! The 19th Division were to complete the capture of La Boisselle by the end of the 4th.

At 9 a.m. on the 4th the 8th Glosters had moved into the support line called Ryecroft Street and at 5 p.m. they moved back into La Boisselle where they occupied the former German dugouts. On the 5th they held the Support Line all day before marching out via the Pozieres-Albert Road. They arrived at billets close to the railway station at Albert. Apart from their loss of six officers killed they also had fourteen wounded and the casualties amongst the other ranks were 282.

La Boisselle July 3rd 1916

Carton de Wiarts's citation was published in the *London Gazette* of September 8th 1916 and was as follows:

"For most conspicuous bravery, coolness and determination during severe operations of a prolonged nature. It was owing in a great measure to his dauntless courage and inspiring example that a serious reverse was averted.

He displayed the utmost energy and courage in forcing our attack home. After three other battalion Commanders had become casualties, he controlled their commands, and ensured that the ground won was maintained at all costs.

He frequently exposed himself in the organisation of positions and of supplies, passing unflinchingly through fire barrage of the most intense nature.

His gallantry was inspiring to all."

Carton de Wiart was presented his V.C. by the King at Buckingham Palace on November 29th 1916.

Carton de Wiart was the son of a Belgian lawyer Leon Carton de Wiart and was born on May 5th 1880. One of his cousins was Count Henri Carton de Wiart, a one time Prime Minister, and another was a Political Secretary to King Leopold II. In Adrian's childhood his father went to Egypt to practice law and became a naturalised British subject. Adrian came to England and went to school at the Oratory School where he was the captain of most of the school sports. He then went up to Balliol College, Oxford and had only been there a short time when the Boer War began.

Carton de Wiart enlisted as a Private serving as a Trooper in the Middlesex Yeomanry (Duke of Cambridge's Hussars) in 1899, and served in South Africa. He was wounded twice and received the Queen's Medal with three clasps. Later

he was commisioned in the 4th Dragoon Guards in 1901, and became a Lieutenant in 1914. He was A.D.C. to the Lieutenant-General, South Africa from July 29th 1905 to October 21st 1905 and A.D.C. to the G.O.C. Chief, South Africa from November 1st, 1905 to March 18th 1908. He was made a Captain in 1910 and became Adjutant with the Gloucestershire Yeomanry from January 1912 to July 1914 when he left for Somaliland where he joined the Camel Corps until March 1915. It was during this period of his career that he lost an eye. He was Mentioned in Despatches and awarded the D.S.O. for distinguished service in the field against the Dervish Forces at Shimber Beris, Somaliland. Carton de Wiart had married the Contessa Frederica Fuger in 1908 by whom he had two daughters.

Carton de Wiart was 34 years of age when the Great War began and he rejoined the 4th Dragoons in Flanders. Almost immediately he was wounded in the left hand which had to be amputated. After leave for this operation he returned to France, and transferred to the Loyal North Lancs Battalion and then took command of the 8th Glosters who were both part of the 19th Division.

After winning the V.C. at La Boisselle, his battalion was one of the very many units who were sent to capture the German held High Wood on the Somme. In this action he was wounded in the skull and was taken down from the dressing station by barge to Corbie. After convalescence he returned again to France and his battalion, and found himself once more near High Wood where he recovered his stick which he had left when wounded! Later he was wounded again by a shell splinter and after sick leave, was given the command

of the 8th North Staffs who went into the line opposite Hebuterne. He later took command of the 12th Bde. of the 4th Division which was involved in the Arras fighting in April 1917 and later in the fight for the Passchendaele Ridge. He was wounded twice more and posted to a Bantam Division. After the Armistice he was given a Brigade in the 38th Div. He had probably been one of the youngest Allied Brigadier-Generals.

In February 1919 he was sent to Poland to head the British Military Mission and stayed in the country for twenty years, before the coming of the Second World War meant a return to England. Once back home he was given the command of the 61st Div. in which the 7th Glosters were serving. He was sent in command of a force to Norway in April 1940 which was given the impossible task of capturing Trondheim. A year later he was off to Jugoslavia in order to head his third Military Mission. Unfortunately his Wellington aeroplane suffered loss of engine power and came down off the Libyan coast. Carton de Wiart had to swim for his life and was subsequently captured by the Italians. He was kept captive near Florence and tried to escape but was recaptured. In August 1943 he was allowed free in order to represent Italy in Lisbon with their surrender negotiations. He then returned to England. In October he went to China as Mr Churchill's personal representative to General Chiang Kai-shek. He was three years in China but while there had a fall which damaged his back and he subsequently spent seven months in hospital.

He was given an Honorary MA at Oxford University in December 1947 and a similar degree at Aberdeen University.

Portrait by Sir W. Orpen 1916

His wife died in 1949 and he married Mrs Joan Sutherland in 1951 and went to live in Ireland at the age of 71. He bought Aghinagh House in Killinardrish, County Cork and stayed in Galway while the house was being repaired. He had published his ,autobiography called *Happy Odyssey* in 1950 and had not had the aid of any notes or diaries as they had been left behind in Poland in 1939. He occasionally travelled to London for service reunions and died in Ireland on June 5th 1963 at the age of 83. In the following month a Requiem Mass was held at Westminster Cathedral and three survivors from the fighting at La Boisselle in July 1916 attended.

Marriage to Mrs Joan Sutherland

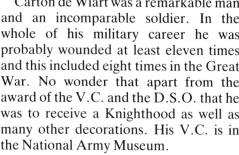

Carton de Wiart was a remarkable man and an incomparable soldier. In the whole of his military career he was probably wounded at least eleven times and this included eight times in the Great War. No wonder that apart from the award of the V.C. and the D.S.O. that he was to receive a Knighthood as well as many other decorations. His V.C. is in the National Army Museum.

Grave and memorial at Killinardrish, Co. Cork. The four sculptured blocks from left to right represent the woodcock, the 4th Dragoon Guards, the V.C. and the duck

Move to Killinardrish, Co. Cork

T. G. Turrall

On July 2nd/3rd apart from the V.C. awarded to Carton de Wiart of the 8th Glosters, the award was also given to Private Thomas George Turrall of the 10th Worcesters which was another battalion serving with the 57th Bde. of the 19th (Western Division).

On July 2nd 1916, the 58th Bde. (19th Div.) attacked the strongly fortified village of La Boisselle and secured a position on the southern face. As the German machine guns were very active it was decided to continue the attack in the night and the 57th Bde. were given this

La Boisselle July 3rd 1916

task. The troops formed up opposite the village and had to endure a terrific bombardment. The order to advance was given at 3am and the attack went forward. Despite the heavy shelling the 10th Worcesters crossed the open ground and into the German defensive positions. The enemy had the advantage of numerous dugouts and machine gun nests and kept appearing. There was heavy hand to hand fighting and the battle became very confused. In the fierce fighting the Colonel (G. A. Royston-Piggott), the Adjutant and all the rest of the senior battalion officers were either killed or wounded. Control became impossible and the fighting was left to small groups of men. The fighting went on until dawn and by this time most of the enemy strongholds had been cleared.

Before the battle began Private Turrall had been serving a short sentence in the

Gallahers Cigarette Card

battalion guardroom, however his platoon officer Lt. Richard William Jennings had decided to set Turrall free in order to allow him to take part in the fighting. Turrall was a powerfully built man and a noted character in the battalion. Both men had a healthy respect for each other's qualities. When it grew lighter the small group under Jennings' leadership was suddenly fired upon from a hidden German position. Jennings was severely wounded and had one of his legs shattered by bullets. Turrall took charge of the situation and dragged his officer into the safety of the nearby shell hole, he then began to dress Jennings' wounds. He used part of an entrenching tool as a splint and one of his own puttees for a bandage. While he worked several bombs were thrown as the enemy had seen movement in the shell hole. The bombers were concealed behind a hedge and Turrall managed to kill at least one of them with rifle fire and the enemy withdrew. However his troubles were not yet over as he could see that there was a mass of Germans attempting to re-take the village in a strong counter-attack. His officer had fainted and there was no point in shooting and so he feigned death, he was prodded with bayonets but survived. The enemy counter-attack against the British defences was broken.

Turrall had to remain until dark in his shell hole and then hoisting up his wounded officer he dragged him back towards the British lines. Jennings was a very tall man and his arms were around Turrall's neck and his feet dragged along behind him. The two men were challenged and this was Turrall's worst moment of the day. "Halt! Hands up!" and Turrall complied, "That man behind you too. Quick!" However Turrall's English voice was recognised and the two

men were allowed back into their lines.

Jennings was able to give a full report on Turrall's bravery but unfortunately his wounds were to prove mortal and he died a few hours later at Dernancourt field dressing station, some accounts say that he died 48 hours later but this is not so. His body was taken to Meaulte Military Cemetery to the south of Albert where it is buried in Row D Grave 34. Jennings, who had been Mentioned in Despatches was the son of a Gloucestershire Parson from Stonehouse. He had been a boxing champion while at Cambridge University and had trained to become a Solicitor. He was 27 when he died of wounds.

The Worcesters were relieved by the 7th South Lancashire Bn. of the 56th Bde. The Worcesters rested in the reserve position known as "Ryecroft Avenue." On the 4th they moved up in

At Buckingham Palace with his daughter

support at La Boisselle but were relieved after a few hours and retired to the Tara-Usna Line before leaving the battlefield with the rest of the 57th Bde. for billets in Albert.

Turrall's V.C. was published in the *London Gazette* of September 9th 1916 and was as follows:

"For most conspicuous bravery and devotion to duty. During a bombing attack by a small party against the enemy the officer in charge was badly wounded, and the party having penetrated the position to a great depth was compelled eventually to retire.

Private Turrall remained with the wounded officer for three hours, under continuous and very heavy fire from machine guns and bombs, and, not withstanding that both himself and the officer were at one time completely cut off from our troops, he held to his ground with determination, and finally carried the officer into our lines after our counter-attacks had made this possible."

He went with his parents and his baby daughter to Buckingham Palace to receive his award on December 30th 1916.

———

Turrall was the son of Mr and Mrs Turrall of 23, Oakley Road, Small Heath, Birmingham. He was born on July 5th 1885. As a child he attended the Dixon Road School and later trained to be a decorator. He joined the 10th Worcesters in 1915 when he was in his 30th year. After the award of his V.C. was announced, two thousand residents in the region of his home assembled at Small Heath Park to present him with £250 which they had contributed to together with a gold watch. He was the third Birmingham citizen to gain the V.C. and received congratulations from the Lord Mayor who was Neville Chamberlain.

April 1964 ("The Firm")

He was presented with a commissioned portrait of himself.

In 1932 a Birmingham local paper carried a picture of Tom Turrall painting railings. He used to attend many regimental functions and was often the guest of honour. He also attended many of the V.C. and G. C. Reunions. He became a well known and respected local figure in Worcestershire and the Midlands.

On February 19th 1964 two days before died he received a visit from two Lieutenant Colonels from the Regiment who found him in 'very good cheer'. Two days later he died in Sally Oak Hospital, Birmingham at the age of 78. He was given a full military funeral at the Robin Hood Cemetery, Solihull, Warwickshire and there was a large attendance. His coffin was draped in the Union Jack and buglers played the *Last Post* and *Reveille*. A pall bearing party of eight men was supplied from the Brigade Depot at Lichfield. After his death his six medals were left to the Regiment.

T. O. L. Wilkinson

Lieut. T. O. L. WILKINSON, V.C.

Gallahers Cigarette Card

In the early days of July 1916 the 57th Bde. of the 19th (Western) Division earned two Victoria Crosses. On July 5th a member of the 7th L. N. Lancs. who were part of the 56th Bde. in the same Division was also going to earn the highest military award. The name of the man was Lt T. O. L. Wilkinson.

At the end of June on the eve of the battle the 7th L. N. Lancs. were camped at Henencourt Wood and on the 30th went forward to trenches to the north east of Albert. The L. N. Lancs were the reserve battalion to the 8th Div. on the 1st of July and on the 2nd they were relieved

and went back to a railway cutting close to Albert. At 3am on the 3rd they were again on the move and their destination was the Tara-Usna Line on the right of the main Albert-Bapaume Road. The battalion remained there in reserve until night. They were supporting the 7th Royal Lancaster Regiment who were occupying a former German front line trench. At 1.am on the 4th the L. N. Lancs. were ordered to a trench line near La Boisselle. The trench was "very much knocked about and full of dead", fighting was renewed at 8 o'clock in the morning.

On the 3rd the 57th and 58th Bdes. had attacked the village of La Boisselle and on the 4th the village was taken. The L. N. Lancs were involved in this action and about 40-50 prisoners went through their lines. At dusk the fighting began to subside. At 2 p. m. on the 5th the L. N. Lancs. were detailed to help the 7th East Lancs. with a bombing attack, unfortunately the East Lancs. lost ground and fell back to an original British front line position and in doing so left behind a machine gun. The L. N. Lancs. were immediately ordered to recover both the lost ground and the gun which they successfully accomplished. Lt. Wilkinson held some Germans up on the left with the machine gun when they were advancing down a trench. His prompt action prevented a determined rush by the enemy. It was for this deed that he was recommended the V.C. by Lt. Col. Sherbrooke CO of the 1st Sherwood Foresters. Soon after Wilkinson's gallantry however he was killed when trying to rescue a wounded man who was lying forty yards in front of the battalion position The battalion was to remain in

La Boisselle July 5th 1916

the trench line near La Boisselle until late evening on the 7th.

Wilkinson's posthumous award was gazetted on September 26th 1916 and read as follows:

"For most conspicuous bravery. During an attack, when a party of another unit was retiring without their machine gun, Lt. Wilkinson rushed forward and, with two of his men, got the gun into action, and held up the enemy until they were relieved.

Later, when the advance was checked during a bombing attack, he forced his way forward and found four or five men of different units stopped by a solid block of earth, over which the enemy were throwing bombs.

With great pluck and promptness he mounted a machine gun on the top of a parapet and dispersed the enemy bombers. Subsequently he made two most gallant attempts to bring in a wounded man, but in the second attempt he was shot through the heart just before reaching the man.

Throughout the day he set a magnificent example of courage and self-sacrifice."

———

Thomas Orde Lawder Wilkinson was the second son of Mr. C. E. Orde Wilkinson and was born at The Lodge Farm, Dudmaston, Bridgnorth, Shropshire on June 29th 1891. His father was in Comax, Vancouver at the time of his younger son's birth, and Thomas visited Vancouver Island in 1913 and enlisted with the first Canadian Contingent on August 4th 1914 and came to England with them. He was recommended for a commission with the L. N. Lancs. in January 1915 and went with them to France in 1916.

Thiepval Memorial (D. C. Jennings)

Wilkinson's father collected his son's posthumous V.C. from the King at Buckingham Palace on November 29th 1916.

Wilkinson's body was never found and his name is therefore listed on the Thiepval Memorial to the missing, Pier and Face 11A. His Regiment possesses his wallet which contains two letters to his parents and also the original citation written by Lt. Col. Sherbrooke. His medals are in private hands.

D. S. Bell

To the south east of La Boisselle the objective to be given to the 69th Bde. of the 23rd Div. was to capture a position that was was known as Horseshoe Trench which ran from Lincoln Redoubt to Scots' Redoubt. It was a position that was about 1500 yards long and stood on high ground in a slight curve between La Boisselle and Mametz Wood. The 69th Bde. consisted of four battalions, the 11th W. Yorks, the 10th D.W.R. and the 8th and 9th Green Howards. It is the last unit that we are most concerned with as one of its officers was Sec. Lt. D. S. Bell. Before the battle started the 9th Green Howards had been waiting in the village of St. Sauveur which was in the valley of the River Somme to the south of the battlefield. On the 1st of July they marched at night to some woods to the west of the village of Baizieux where they camped and heard rumours of how the fighting for La Boisselle had been going and of the enormous casualties suffered by the 8th and 34th Divisions. A day later the Green Howards marched up to billets on the fringe of the battle area just outside the town of Albert. They moved up the Bapaume Road and reached as far as the Tara-Usna Ridge where they took stock of the situation. They were to take the position on the crest of the ridge to the south-east of La Boisselle. Headquarters was established at Chapes Spur. On the 4th, bombing attacks were made by the battalion and the West Yorks. and the enemy fought back with great determination. On the 5th an attack was made at dawn by the West Yorks. and the 10th D.W.R. but a German counter attack nullified any progress and the Yorshiremen ended up at their original lines. Another attempt was made by these two battalions in the afternoon. Orders were issued for the two Green Howard Battalions to enter the battle but as there had

D. S. Bell

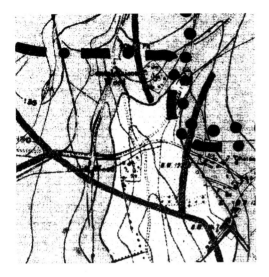

been some progress on the right only the 9th Battalion was called upon. The time was 6 p.m. and despite several officers becoming casualties great progress was made and Horseshoe Trench was not only taken but 146 prisoners were

captured as well as two enemy machine guns. However a German machine gun began to enfilade the Yorkshire Battalion's position and it was seeing this that prompted 2nd Lt. Bell, supported by Cpl. Colwill and Pte. Batey to try and destroy the gun position. The three men crept towards it using a communication trench, and then suddenly dashed across the open, Bell shot the gunner with his

Signpost to Gordon Dump Cemetery
(P. Batchelor)

revolver and the remainder of the gun team were killed by bombs. The German position was clearly not ready for such a brazenly frontal attack and was overwhelmed by the speed of Bell's thinking and deeds as much as anything. The citation for the V.C. was published on September 9th 1916 and read as follows:

"For most conspicuous bravery. During an attack a very heavy enfilade fire was opened on the attacking company by a hostile machine gun. 2nd Lt. Bell immediately, and on his own initiative, crept up a communication trench and then, followed by Cpl. Colwill and Pte. Batey, rushed across the open under very heavy fire and attacked the machine gun, shooting the firer with his revolver, and destroying gun and personnel with bombs.

Horseshoe Trench July 5th 1916

This very brave act saved many lives and ensured the success of the attack. Five days later this gallant officer lost his life performing a very similar act of bravery."

On the 6th it was raining hard and the 69th Bde. was relieved in the front line but there was little respite for the men. The village of Contalmaison was the objective and Bell was killed in fighting on July 10th to the south east of the village, at the time he was attached to the 8th Green Howards. After his death Horseshoe Trench was renamed Bell's Redoubt. Bell was buried where he fell and his body was later transferred to Gordon Dump Cemetery (IV, A, 8).

Donald Simpson Bell was the younger son of Mr and Mrs Smith Bell of, 87, East Parade, Harrogate and was born on December 3rd 1890. Throughout his life he was to be known as Donny. He was educated at St Peter's School, Harrogate

87 East Parade, Harrogate

Gordon Dump Cemetery (D. C. Jennings)

where he gained a scholarship. He went on to Knaresborough Grammar School and from there to Westminster College. He had a very strongly built physique and by the age of sixteen he was already six foot tall and weighed over fourteen stone. Not surprisingly he was very good at sports and although his was more the build of a hammer-thrower than a runner, he did still possess an amazing turn of speed that he brought into good use when he gained the V.C. When still at school he played full back for Starbeck Football Club and when he became a teacher at Westminster he turned out for Crystal Palace. On returning north he played for Bradford Park Avenue. Some of these clubs paid him and this supplement helped to eke out his teacher's salary which never exceeded £2.50 per week. He also played Rugby and Cricket. He was an Assistant Master at Starbeck Council School, near Harrogate before joining up with the Yorkshire Regiment as a Private in November 1914. He obtained his commission in June 1915. A year later on June 5th 1916 he married Rhoda Margaret Bonson at Kirkby Stephen, it was a marriage that was barely to last five weeks.

We are very fortunate in that a letter dated July 7th from Bell to his mother has survived. In it he talks about his role in the fighting for the Horseshoe position on the 5th of July the letter 'fleshes out' the standard prose of the official citation. ". . . . . As I told you, the battalion had been in action and did splendidly capturing a strong German position. I did not go over as I was second in command of the bombers. . . . . a machine gun was spotted on the left, which could enfilade the whole of the front. When the battalion went over, I with my team, crawled up a communication trench and attacked the gun and the trench and I hit the gun first shot from about 20 yards and knocked it over. We then bombed the dug-outs and did in about 50 Bosches. The G.O.C. has been over to congratulate the battalion and he personally thanked me. I must confess that it was the biggest fluke alive and I did nothing. I only chucked one bomb, but it did the trick. . . . . I am glad I have been so fortunate, for Pa's sake, for I know he likes his lads to be at the top of the tree. He used to be always on about too much play and too little work, but my athletics came in handy this trip. . . . . The only thing is I am sore at elbows and knees with crawling over limestone flints etc. . . . . believe that God is watching over me and it rests with him whether I pull through or not. I will write again as soon

as I get another chance and will send Field P. C's every day if possible. . . . ."

On September 16th after the V.C. award had been announced Brig. Gen. T. S. Lambert, Commander of the 69th Bde. wrote a congratulatory letter to Bell's father. Colonel H. G. Holmes and Major H. A. S. Prior wrote in similar fashion to Bell's widow, who as a registered reader of the Daily Mail was given £100 by that newspaper. However by far the most moving of these letters was one from Bell's batman to Mrs Bell, who had presumably written to him to ask of more personal details about her husband's last days in early July 1916.

The letter was dated November 14th and reads as follows:

". . . I sit down and write these few lines in deepest regret, believe me I am most sorry that it should be so. I would to God that my late master and friend had still been here with us, or better still, been at home with you, ... They (the company) worshipped him in their simple, whole hearted way and so they ought, he saved the lot of us from being completely wiped out, by his heroic act. . . . . . I am pleased that his valise arrived to you and that you think it is allright, you would find in it the souvenirs that we got on the 5th of July in the first great attack, a Prussian helmet, bayonet and pair of boots. . I packed them all in it but I cannot quite remember whether his little toilet bag was packed, or he carried it with him at the time of his death. . . . . . he was called to go to the 8th Battalion of this regiment, that was just on our right, so that we heard nothing of his death until the next day. . . . The last time we were on the Somme, some of our lads came across Mr Bell's grave and they told me that it was being well cared for, and that there is a cross erected over it, ... You ask me if I smoke, yes, but not cigarettes, only a pipe and tobacco so if you will send some, I will be very grateful to you. Believe me, wishing you the best of health and wishes,

Yours in Sympathy, John W. Byers.
(Private John W. Byers, C. Co. 9th Batt. Yorks Regt., B.E.F.)"

Colonel A. C. T. White, V.C., M. C. not only attended the same school as Bell but was also a sportsman and a member of the Green Howards. Some years later when writing to the Regimental Magazine he said this of Bell's deed:

"At Contalmaison the problem was to cross No Man's Land, badly cut up by shell fire. Probably no one else on the front could have done what he (Bell) did.

Laden by steel helmet, haversack, revolver, ammunitions and Mills bombs in their pouches, he was yet able to hurl himself at the German trench at such speed that the enemy would hardly believe what their eyes saw.

Well knowing the risk, he made a similar attempt a few days later, and died. He was a magnificent soldier; and had he lived, with his high intelligence. superb physique, and firm religious principles, he would have risen high in the teaching profession."

Bell's life was commemorated at Starbeck Council School, the town memorial at Harrogate, and at St Peters Church Harrogate. His medals are with the Green Howards.

W. E. Boulter

After La Boisselle had fallen the main Allied attacks were made against the German second line positions of Mametz Wood and Trones Wood. The latter wood was like a pear in shape and was to the east of Bernafay Wood and of the village of Montauban. It was a position of vital strategic importance to both sides and was only two miles from the German station at Combles, which was a very important "nerve centre".

By the second week of July Trones Wood had been captured and lost by the British several times. The 30th Division who had been very heavily involved in the fighting were relieved by the 18th (Eastern) Division on the evening of the 12th. Their orders were that the wood must be taken on the 14th and the attack was part of the plan to take the whole of the German Second Line. The attack was to begin at 3.20 am and the 18th Div. had three Brigades, the 53rd, 54th and 55th. At first the 55th occupied the front line

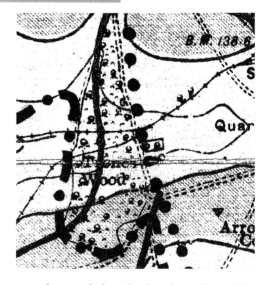

trenches and then had to be relieved by the 54th. One of the four battalions in the 54th was the 6th Northamptons and after very fierce hand-to-hand fighting the wood was finally cleared. It was during this part of the fighting that the first 6th Northamptonshire Battalion V.C. was

Gallahers Cigarette Card

This very gallant act not only saved many casualties, but was of great military value as it materially expedited the operation of clearing the enemy out of the wood, and thus covering the flank of the whole attacking force."

The other battalion who was heavily involved in capturing the wood was the 12th Middlesex and the two battalions were relieved on the 16th. The 6th Northants. had suffered 296 casualties. Boulter received his Victoria Cross from the King at Buckingham Palace on March 17th 1917.

William Ewart Boulter was the son of Frederick and Mary Ann Boulter and was born in Wigston, Leicestershire on October 14th 1892. He was educated at Wigston Council Schools and a keen sportsman. He joined the Northamptonshires at the age of twenty one in September 1914. He was promoted to the rank of Sergeant the following May, and two months later he sailed with the 18th Division to France. The 6th Northants had been formed at Colchester and

won by Sergeant William Boulter. His Citation was published on October 26th 1916 in the *London Gazette* and read as follows:

"For most conspicuous bravery. When a company and part of another were held up in the attack on a wood (Trones) by a hostile machine gun, which was causing heavy casualties, Sergeant Boulter, with utter contempt of danger and in spite of being severely wounded in the shoulder, advanced alone over the open under heavy fire in front of the gun, and bombed the gun team from their position.

Officer Cadet

moved to Salisbury to complete their training. In 1915 the battalion spent their first winter in the trenches at Suzanne and Fricourt, where mining was a constant danger. At the beginning of the Somme battle they were involved in capturing the village of Montauban on the first day. After a short rest the battalion returned to the Somme and were involved in a third success, the capture of Thiepval. Boulter who was seriously wounded on July 14th 1916 was transferred to a hospital in England on the 18th. He was then sent to Ampthill command depot which was under the command of the Duke of Bedford. Boulter was convalescent until March 1917 and at this time was recommended for a commission and transferred to Newmarket. After he had been awarded the V.C. he was given a clock by the Co-Operative Society at a presentation ceremony at Abingdon Park, Northampton, where twenty thousand people attended. The Corporation of Northampton gave him a gold

Trones Wood July 14th 1916

Buckingham Palace March 17th 1917

wrist watch and a congratulatory address. He was gazetted as a Second Lieutenant on June 26th and returned to France two months later, this time with the 7th Northants. In October though, he contracted trench fever and was unable to take an active part in the war anymore. He was promoted to a full Lieutenant on December 27th 1918 and was demobilized on April 24th 1919.

After the war he lived in London for twenty five years and became seriously ill in 1955 when living at 10 Wimbledon Close, The Downs, Wimbledon. He was in hospital for two months before dying on June 1st 1955 at the age of 62. He was cremated at Putney Vale five days later and his ashes were scattered in the Garden of Remembrance on the first lawn between two cherry trees close to a lily pool. His widow was Alice Irene Boulter and at one time he had three brothers living at Wigston, his birthplace.

In 1988 Boulter's family attended a Northamptonshire Regimental Reunion and presented his V.C. to the Regiment.

W. F. Faulds

Gallahers Cigarette Card

Pte. WILLIAM F. FAULDS, V.C.
Photo: Central Press

After Trones and Mametz Woods had been captured by the Allies the next two woods that were to be taken were High to the north-west of Longueval and Delville which was part of Longueval. The main attack on the 15th of July against High Wood failed and the battle of Delville Wood was begun on same day. Waterlot Farm which was to the south of Longueval was captured on the 17th, it was to the north-east of Trones Wood.

On the 15th 121 officers and 3,022 men of the 1st South African Infantry Brigade entered the wood and fought there for almost a week in appalling conditions. They were pinned down by continuous bombardment and were attacked from three sides. Delville Wood was to become the place that was most associated with the South African Forces in the Great War and on the 16th one of their men, Private W.F. Faulds carried out the first of two outstanding acts of gallantry thus gaining the first V.C. for the Imperial forces in the battle of the Somme and also the first V.C. out of four that were to be given for gallantry in this particular action.

Faulds was a company runner and on

the morning of the 16th two companies of the South African Infantry who had been manning the south-west corner of the wood were ordered to push out from Princes Street in order to link up with the 11th Royal Scots. The plan was to capture an orchard but the attack failed. Lt. Arthur Craig (S.A.I.) led a bombing party against the enemy trenches but came under heavy machine gun fire. Most of the party were either killed or wounded and Craig himself was severely wounded. In full view of both sides, Private Faulds, together with Privates George Baker and Alexander Estment climbed over the parapet in order to rescue the wounded officer. One of the party was injured but they still managed to carry Craig back to their trench. Later that day the northern part of the wood was vacated in order to allow it to be bombarded by the Allied artillery. On the 18th Private Faulds again risked his life by going out in order to rescue a wounded man, again under intense enemy fire.

Finally the South Africans who were in the south-west corner of the wood and almost totally depleted were relieved in the early evening of the 20th by men of the 76th Bde. Their number was 142 survivors including two wounded officers and under Colonel Thackeray they left for Happy Valley, a camp close to the town of Bray, on the Somme river to the south.

Faulds' citation was published on September 9th 1916 and read as follows:

"For most conspicuous bravery and devotion to duty. A bombing party under Lt. Craig attempted to rush over 40 yards of ground which lay between the British and enemy trenches. Coming under very heavy rifle and machine gun fire the officer and the majority of the party were killed or wounded. Unable to move, Lieut. Craig lay midway between the two lines of trench, the ground being quite open. In full daylight Private Faulds accompanied by two other men, climbed over the parapet, ran and picked up the officer, and carried him back, one man being severely wounded in so doing. Two days later Private Faulds again showed most conspicuous bravery in going out alone to bring in a wounded man, and carried him nearly half a mile to a dressing station, subsequently rejoining his platoon. The artillery-fire was at the time so intense that stretcher bearers and others considered that any attempt to bring in the wounded man meant certain death. The risk Private Faulds faced unflinchingly, and his bravery was crowned with success."

When Craig was transferred to a Hospital in England he wrote to three members of the Faulds family telling them how Private Faulds had saved his life and that it was a million to one chance that he survived. Craig wrote to Faulds himself thanking him, to his sister and to his mother. Faulds was awarded his V.C.

Delville Wood July 18th 1916

by the King at Sandringham on January 8th 1917.

———————

William Frederick Faulds was born at 34 Market Street, Cradock, Cape Province on February 19th 1895. His parents were Allexander and Wilhelmina Faulds. He went to school at Cradock and worked at the Midland Motor Garage, Cradock before joining the Cradock Commando on October 19th 1914 at the age of nineteen. His mother was a widow with seven children, two of whom were to serve in the S.A.I. Faulds was always known as Mannie. He served in South West Africa throughout the campaign until he was discharged on January 12th 1915. He re-enlisted in the 1st S.A.I. on August 23rd for the duration of the war and arrived in France with them on April 16th 1916.

After news of his V.C. award had reached Johannesburg a cable told him that his award "had sent a thrill of pride throughout the country."

On August 20th 1916 Faulds was promoted to the rank of Lance-Corporal, to Corporal on October 18th 1916, to Sergeant on April 12th 1917. and on May 19th of that year he was commissioned as a Second Lieutenant. He then served for a short time in the Transport in Egypt before returning to France. During the March German breakthrough in 1918 Faulds was reported as being wounded and in German hands. He was awarded the M.C. for his work in handling his men during the German attacks at Heudecourt and this enabled the rest of the battalion to withdraw with only slight losses. He was made Temporary Lieutenant on November 9th 1918 and repatriated to England ten days later.

After the war he returned to South

Cradock, Salisbury, South Africa (I. Uys)

Africa for demobilization and was made a full Lieutenant in March 1919. Two years later he married Thelma M. Windell in Kimberley and they had two children. He became a mechanic with De Beers and in 1922 he re-enlisted with the Kimberley Regiment. He became a Captain and after several years left Kimberley to work in Jagersfontein and then moved to Rhodesia. In 1937 he attended the Coronation of King George VIth and served for five years in the Second World War, mainly in East Africa. In 1945 he became a Government Inspector in Rhodesia and died in Salisbury General Hospital at the age of 55 on August 16th 1951. He was buried in the Salisbury Pioneer Cemetery on August 17th in a grave without a monument or headstone. However in 1972 this was rectified mainly through the efforts of the Cradock branch of the South African Legion. His eleven medals are on display at the South African National Museum of Military History in the Adler Hall.

W. La T. Congreve

Not only Joseph Davies and Albert Hill were to be awarded the V.C. as a result of gallantry on July 20th 1916 but so was William Congreve, but this time post-humously. He was killed to the north west of Delville Wood, at the age of 25. He was Brigade Major of the 76th Bde. of the 3rd Division. His Bde. consisted of the 8th King's Own, 2nd Suffolks, 10th R. W. F. and 1st Gordons. His citation was published in the *London Gazette* dated October 26th 1916 and read as follows:

"For most conspicuous bravery during a period of fourteen days preceding his death in action.

This officer constantly performed acts

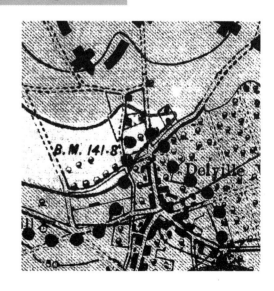

Gallahers Cigarette Card

of gallantry and showed the greatest devotion to duty, and by his personal example inspired all around him with confidence at critical periods of the operations. During preliminary preparations for the attack he carried out personal reconnaissances of the enemy lines, taking out parties of officers and non-commissioned officers for over a 1,000 yards in front of our line, in order to acquaint them with the ground. All these preparations were made under fire.

Later, by night, Major Congreve conducted a battalion to its position of employment, afterwards returning to it to ascertain the situation after assault. He established himself in an exposed forward position from whence he successfully observed the enemy, and gave orders necessary to drive them from their position. Two days later, when Brigade Headquarters was heavily shelled and many casualties resulted, he went out and assisted the medical officer to remove the wounded to places of safety, although he was himself suffering severely from gas and other shell effects. He again on a subsequent occasion showed supreme courage in tending wounded under heavy shell fire.

He finally returned to the front line to ascertain the situation after an unsuccessful attack, and whilst in the act of writing his report, was shot and killed instantly."

He was given the posthumous award for his work over the period July 6th-July 20th in the region of Montauban, Delville Wood, Longueval and the Bazentin Ridge. He was buried at Corbie Communal Cemetery Extension, (I.F.35) . His widow received her husband's medals from the King at Buckingham Palace on November 1st 1916 and they included the D.S.O. and the M.C. as well as the V.C. Congreve was the first officer in the Great War to earn all three medals.

William La Touche Congreve was the son of Lt. Gen. Sir Walter Congreve, V.C., K.C.B., M.V.O., etc and Lady Congreve. He was born on March 22nd 1891 at Burton Hall, Cheshire. He was educated at Eton and Sandhurst where he came second for the Sword of Honour. He was gazetted as a 2nd Lieutenant in the Rifle Brigade in March 1911 and later joined the 3rd Bn. in Tipperary. On February 1st 1913 he became a full Lieutenant and left for France with the 3rd Rifle Bde. on September 12th 1914. He became

Longueval July 20th 1916

A.D.C. to Major Gen. Hubert Hamilton who was commander of the 3rd Division until he was killed by shrapnel on October 14th and then to Hamilton's successor, Major Gen. J. A. L. Haldane. He continued to serve the 3rd Div. as a General Staff Officer and as Bde. Major to the

Corbie Communal Cemetery Ext. (C.W.G.C.)

76th Bde.

He was mentioned in despatches four times before his death and once afterwards. He was awarded the M.C. on January 14th 1916 for bravery at Hooge in 1915. On February 24th he was given the award of the *Legion of Honour* and on April 6th he was recommended for the V.C. for the first time but was given the D.S.O. on April 22nd instead. The exploit took place at the end of March in the region of St. Eloi in Belgium, he and his orderly went up to a huge mine crater and captured two officers and 72 men of the Prussian Army. Congreve had crept up to the crater and brandishing his revolver ordered the garrison to surrender. The mines had been sprung by the British on March 26th. It was during this period that the Rev. Noel Mellish earned the V.C. for saving the lives of several

Corbie Communal Cemetery Ext. (D. C. Jennings)

They entered the front line trench along side Dukes Street which was on the west side of Longueval. It was when making notes of the situation that a sniper shot Congreve in the throat when he was climbing down from the top of a disused gunpit. The sniper had been hidden by stooks of corn. The time of death was 10. 55am. The next day Congreve's body was taken to Corbie via Carnoy. His father had to attend a Fourth Army Conference and afterwards visited the body of his dead son and kissed him goodbye.

Congreve was very highly thought of and loved by his men. One member of the Rifle Bde. says this of him:

"He was the most perfect gentleman and the coolest officer in the British

men over a period of three successive nights in the same sector. In June 1916 he was given his Brevet-Majority. On the 1st of the same month he married Pamela Maude an actress and daughter of Cyril Maude. The wedding took place at St. Martin's-in-the-Fields.

On July 20th the fighting to capture Longueval and Delville Wood was still the main priority and two battalions of the 76th Bde. were involved, the 2nd Suffolks and the 10th. R.W.F. The Suffolks began their advance from the westerly direction at 3.35 am and the R.W.F. failed to make contact as they were led astray by guides who lost their way. The Suffolks went on unsupported and were decimated. When the 10th R.W.F. did finally arrive they were mistakenly fired on by the 11th Essex battalion. It was this mess that Congreve was attempting to sort out when he talked to Major Stubbs at the Suffolk's H.Q.

Walter Congreve

Army. He was beloved by all. . . .
Everyone grieved his loss, and none more
so than his devoted orderly who broke
down in tears on news of his master's
death."   He was recommended the
V.C. on the second occasion by Brig.
Gen R. J. Kentish commanding officer of
the 76th Bde. Major-Gen. Haldane,
Commander of the 3rd Div. with whom
Congreve had served 20 months wrote
this of him:
    "His loss to me is irreparable, and the
Army in him loses one of its very best
soldiers and by far the most promising
officer I have ever known. Young, almost
boyish in appearance, he possessed
qualities which are generally found only
in men of much riper years and of far
greater experience. He was unsurpassed
in bravery, and was distinguished by the
highest standards of duty which guided
him. Had he lived but a few months

W. La T. Congreve

longer he must inevitably have attained
command of a Brigade. Under his
modesty and gentleness he possessed
great strength of character. The whole
Division mourns his loss, for he was
beloved by all ranks, and the fine
example he set of duty well done will for
long keep him alive in their memories."
In a letter to Congreve's widow which is
quoted in his diary published under
the title of *Armageddon Road A VC's
Diary 1914-1916* Haldane also wrote
as follows: "I am so upset at what has
happened that writing is difficult. Still
I must write and say how infinitely sorry I
am for you and how deeply sad I feel. . . .
On the 18th, when things were not going
too well, and I had been obliged to use
the 76th Bde. - which I was preserving for
another operation-I went through the
ruined village of Montauban into the

Lady Congreve

Pamela Maude (Mrs Congreve) (Country Life)

valley south of Longueval, where the headquarters of the brigade were in a quarry. The enemy was very active, shelling heavily, and Billy had just returned from a dangerous visit to Longueval and gave me a lucid and manly account of what was going on there, I mean reassuring under the circumstances. He looked tired, but I knew that if I said he was overworking he would scorn the idea. That was the last time I saw him alive. Cameron, his faithful servant is heartbroken. . . . . I took one look at the dear fellow, (Congreve). He looked beautiful in his last sleep, so handsome and noble, and not a trace of pain on his face. He was then half-way to Carnoy and, on my way back there, I met men of my regiment (Gordon Highlanders) carrying wild poppies and cornflowers to lay upon him, for his love for his brigade was

amply returned by all ranks."

Congreve's father Walter Congreve was also the holder of the V.C. which he won at the Battle of Colenso, South Africa in 1899. There had only been two other occasions where father and son had both been awarded the V.C. William Congreve's mother also received the French Croix de Guerre in recognition of her work as a nurse in the Nancy area.

On March 21st 1917 Pamela Congreve gave birth to a daughter named Gloria and on December 22nd 1919 Pamela married Major the Hon. William Fraser, D.S.O., M.C. the third surviving son of Lord Saltoun at St Georges. Hanover

Mrs. La Touche Congreve, formerly Miss Pamela Maude, widow of Major La Touche Congreve, V.C., who was killed in action within a few weeks of his wedding, yesterday at St. George's, Hanover-square, was married to Major William Fraser. The bride-groom, who was best man to Major Congreve, is son of Lord Saltoun.—(Daily Sketch.)

Mrs W. La T. Congreve and the Hon. W. Fraser

Stow-by-Chartley Church, Staffs. (D. Gillard)

father's seven medals up for sale as she wanted the money in order to buy a house in Spain. The medals had been on display at the Green Jackets Museum. There was an uproar in the press and Congreve's brother Christopher was particularly upset. An appeal was launched by which the Royal Green Jackets Museum of Winchester would be able to buy the medals. The Rifle Bde. had been amalgamated under the banner of the Royal Green Jackets. The price expected for the medals was between £15,000 and £21,000 and in the end the Museum bought the set for £26,000.

Congreve is commemorated on the panels of the Rifle Brigade Memorial in Winchester Cathedral and at Stow-by-Chartley church Staffordshire. Walter Congreve also has a plaque to his memory at Stow. William also has a plaque to his memory in Corbie Abbey close to where he is buried.

Square. He had been a great friend of Billy's and had been best man at his wedding and had commanded the 1st Gordons during the last few months of the war. The Gordons, it will be remembered had been part of the 76th Bde.

On June 30th 1983 Gloria put her

Stow-by-Chartley Church, Staffs. (D. Gillard)

A LA MÉMOIRE GLORIEUSE
DU COMMANDANT
WILLIAM LA TOUCHE CONGREVE
DU RIFLE BRIGADE, DE L'ARMÉE BRITANNIQUE,
CHEVALIER DE LA LÉGION D'HONNEUR,
DÉCORÉ DE LA VICTORIA CROSS DU
DISTINGUISHED SERVICE ORDER ET
DE LA MILITARY CROSS.

HOMME SANS PEUR, SOLDAT VAILLANT,
IL TOMBA AU CHAMP D'HONNEUR LE 20
JUILLET 1916 À LONGUEVALLE, SOMME
A L'ÂGE DE 25 ANS A L'AURORE D'UNE
BRILLANTE CARRIÈRE, AIMÉ DE TOUS.

Il repose à Corbie

Corbie Church, France.

J. J. Davies

J. J. Davies

Two days after the South African Private Faulds gained the V.C. for gallantry in the fighting for Delville Wood two members of the 10th Royal Welch Fusiliers were also to qualify for the British Army's top award. Their names were Joseph Davies and Albert Hill and the date was July 20th 1916.

The 10th R.W.F. were part of the 76th Bde. of the 3rd Division. Other battalions in their brigade were the 8th King's Own, 2nd Suffolks and 1st Gordons. The Division was ordered to capture the village of Longueval and the adjacent Delville Wood. Only the southern part of the wood was in Allied hands and the 2nd Suffolks were ordered to attack Longueval from the west. The 10th R.W.F. who

had started from Montauban and who had reached the wood at 2.45 a.m. were then to push through the wood to the north from a ride in the centre of the wood which was named Princes Street. As so many troops were involved in such a small area the order was given that there should be no firing. The Suffolks went off at 3 a.m. and were not seen again and the R.W.F. were misled by incorrect directions being given to them by the 53rd Bde. They were guided to Buchanan Street, a ride to the south west of Princes Street and suddenly the whole wood seemed to be full of Germans and the Welshmen had great difficulty in finding their way to the centre of the wood.

It was in the middle of the wood and between two German attacking lines that Cpl. Davies was to gain his V.C. He had become separated from his Company (D) which was the leading company and along with eight men he was surrounded. They took cover in a shell hole and by bombing the enemy and using rapid fire managed to repulse their attackers. He then followed up the retreating party of Germans and bayoneted several of them. Then all went quiet and his group deployed to make another attack, all the officers had become casualties and Davies took charge and led the men forward but they were fired upon from all directions. He returned for another group and led them into the attack, the Germans were only 50 yards away and the firing was so intense that Davies' party had to retire 150 yards. Davies kept a tight control of the reserves in the trenches before they were relieved. Owing to the very confusing state of the position the R.W.F. were mistakenly

Delville Wood July 20th 1916

fired on by the 11th Essex and they suffered further casualties. The total casualties of the R.W.F. were 180 including 50 missing and they were relieved on the 21st and spent four days at Breslau Trench before marching back to camp at Bois des Tailles.

Davies' citation was published in the *London Gazette* of September 26th 1916, and read as follows:

"For most conspicuous bravery. Prior to an attack on the enemy in a wood he became separated with eight men from the rest of his company. When the enemy delivered their second counter attack his party was completely surrounded, but he got them into a shell hole, and, by throwing bombs and opening rapid fire, succeeded in routing them. Not content with this he followed them up in their retreat and bayoneted several of them.

Cpl. Davies set a magnificent example of pluck and determination. He had done other very gallant work, and was badly wounded in the second battle of Ypres."

Four days after his V.C. was gazetted he was presented with the medal's ribbon at Enquin-les-Mines by the Commanding Officer of the 76th Bde. Brigadier R. J. Kentish. A week later he was given the medal itself by the King at Buckingham Palace on October 7th. As Davies had been badly wounded in the shoulder in Delville Wood the King had to pin the medal on his sling.

———

Joseph John Davies was the son of John and Annie Davies and was born on April 28th 1889 at Tipton, Staffordshire. The family lived at 48 Cross Street, Wednes-

Gallahers Cigarette Card

fighting at Ypres in 1915 when Davies was wounded for the first time. In July he was wounded a second time when the knuckles of both hands were smashed by German bayonets. In August he was posted to the 1st Garrison Battalion, R.W.F. and served briefly in Gibraltar. He transferred to the 3rd R.W.F. in May 1916 and was promoted to the rank of Corporal, and then Sergeant. He then returned to the 3rd R.W.F. In May 1917 he was transferred to the Military Provost Staff, as his wounds made him unfit for active duty. In the same year he married Elsie Thomas of Presteigne, Herefordshire. (Powys), they were to have two daughters. He was discharged on December 14th 1918, and served briefly in the Herefordshire Regiment. Due to his severe injuries that he sustained during the Great War he was unable to return to his former job at the Colliery, and was employed for a time as a Commissionaire by Birmingham Corporation Gasworks. He then moved to Poole, in Dorset where he worked at the Holton Heath Cordite Factory. During the Second World War, he served as a Regimental Sergeant Major with Poole Cadet Force and at the same time was Chief Warden at Oakdale in Poole. He lived at 11 North Road, Parkstone, Poole before moving to Milne Road, Waterloo, Poole. His last address was 2 Trinidad House, Parkstone, Poole. He died in Bournemouth Hospital, Hampshire on February 16th 1976 at the age of 86. He was cremated in Bournemouth on February 25th, there was no service and his ashes were scattered in the sea off Poole. He had suffered from severe arthritis for many years. His medals included the D.C.M. and the Russian Royal Grand Cross of St. George, First Class, and his name is commemorated at Great Bridge School,

bury which no longer exists as the site has been redeveloped. He went to school at Great Bridge Council School, Tipton and became a colliery worker. He joined the Army at the age of 20 on August 19th 1909, in the 1st Welsh Regiment. He served in Egypt from January 18th 1910 until January 27th 1914. He spent a year of this time with the Camel Corps. He served in India between January 28th and November 17th 1914. His father was also in the Army serving with the 7th Royal Fusiliers.

After the war began the 1st Welsh returned from India and were involved in

J. J. Davies left and Mr W. A. Jones (Regt Museum)

Tipton and at Davies Court, Hightown, Wrexham in North Wales. His V.C. is in the possession of the R.W.F. Museum at Caernarfon Castle, Caernarfon.

A. Hill

At the time that Cpl. Davies was winning a V.C. while fighting with D. Company of the 10th R.W.F. Albert Hill was fighting with C Company of the same battalion and this was to be the third V.C. awarded during the battle to capture Delville Wood.

The citation for Hill's gallantry on July 20th was published on September 26th in the *London Gazette* and read as follows:

"For most conspicuous bravery. When the battalion had deployed under very heavy fire for an attack on the enemy in a wood (Delville) he dashed forward, when the order to charge was given, and, meeting two of the enemy suddenly, bayoneted them both. He was sent later by his platoon sergeant to get in touch with the company, and finding himself cut off and almost surrounded by some twenty of the enemy, attacked them with bombs, killing and wounding many and scattering the remainder.

He then joined a sergeant of his company and helped him find the way back to the lines. When he got back, hearing that his Company Officer and a scout were lying out wounded, he went out and assisted in bringing in the wounded officer, two other men bringing in the scout.

Finally, he himself captured and brought in as prisoners two of the enemy. His conduct throughout was magnificent."

He had been recommended the V.C.

Gallahers Cigarette Card

through the Somme fighting. Many medals, including two V.C.s were given on the field. It was a glorious day; all units had their field kitchens out and we lunched in the open, marching past the General afterwards."

Lummis who was a Lieutenant with the 2nd Suffolks at the time was on leave. He was also on leave when his battalion were involved in the Delville Wood fighting, a factor that possibly saved his life.

The King presented the V.C. medal to Hill at Buckingham Palace on November 18th 1916. In March 1918 Hill was briefly Lummis' orderly when the latter was acting Quartermaster with the 2nd Suffolks.

———

Albert Hill was the son of Harry and Elizabeth Hill and was born in Hulme, Manchester on May 24th 1895. He was one of ten children, six boys and four girls. His family moved to 7 Peacock

Delville Wood July 20th 1916

by his Sergeant, Hugh Green and his commanding officer Captain Scales. He was presented with his V.C. ribbon at the same time as Cpl. J. Davies at Enquin-les-Mines, France by Brig. Gen. R. J. Kentish, D.S.O. on September 30th 1916 which was the day that Kentish left the 76th Bde. Of the ceremony Lt. C. J. Hupfield (2nd Suffolks) wrote to Canon W. M. Lummis:

"I arrived at Enquin-les-Mines in pitch darkness (Sept. 29th). Next day there was a battalion parade and later the whole brigade was drawn up to bid good-bye to its General Kentish, who had led it

Street, Denton (nr. Manchester) in 1907. His father who worked in the colliery at Ashton Moss died soon after and the family moved to a cottage at 45 High Street, Denton. Albert went to school at Trinity Wesleyan School, Denton and after he left school he began work at the Alpha Mill. He then became apprenticed to a very large local firm of hat makers called Joseph Wilson and Sons. He was a member of the planking department.

Illuminated Address

A. Hill

He enlisted at the age of 19 with the R.W.F. on August 3rd 1914 and served in France and Flanders although as he was not only small but slight his family thought that he would be rejected for active service. Two of his brothers also enlisted. On October llth 1916 after he had been presented with his V.C. ribbon but before the King had given him the

actual medal, Hill arrived back at Denton from the trenches. He was given a huge local welcome and thousands of people turned out to greet their 'local hero'. The huge crowd sang songs and hymns including "See the Conquering Hero Comes." He was received by the Mayor and presented with an Illuminated Address and then carried shoulder high to his widowed mother's house in the High Street. His mother waited for him with tears in her eyes. At the door of the cottage was a crowd of children and Hill swooped down on one of his nieces and carried her into the cottage where she sat on his knee while he talked to his friends. At the time he had the reputation of being one of the youngest and the smallest V.C. winner. He was also known as Denton's

Denton, June 1953

V.C. and the Hatters' V.C. He was demobilized in February 1919 and married Doris May Wilson of Hyde, Cheshire a year later on February 14th 1920. He had made his own hat as part of the bridal array. He had resumed work at Wilsons but in 1923 he and his wife emigrated to the United States. He lived in Central Falls before moving to Pawtucket, Rhode Island where he worked as a building labourer with a construction company until he retired. He lived at 41 Thornley Street Pawtucket, 117 Maryland Avenue and finally at 175 Broad Street, Pawtucket. He and his wife had one son and three daughters and seven grand children. At the outbreak of the Second War he had travelled to Canada in order to re-enlist but had been told that his work as a construction worker would be of more use to the war effort. He was given the Coronation Medals in 1937 and 1953. For the latter he was invited to England for the Coronation celebrations, he and his wife had been planning a return visit anyway, before the invitation arrived. They had good seats for the Coronation procession itself on June 2nd 1953 and also spent a week in Hyde and Denton seeing relatives and being received by the Mayor of Denton. When at Hyde Townhall Mr and Mrs Hill were officially welcomed and Hill was given a special tie pin with the local coat of arms on it. The Mayor of Hyde had also been a Hatter. At Denton they were also officially welcomed and were shown a book of press cuttings about Hill's life.

Hill died at the Memorial Hospital, Pawtucket on February 17th 1971 at the age of 75 and was buried three days later at Highland Memorial Park, Pawtucket

with full military honours. His name is commemorated like Joseph Davies in that there is a Court named after him in Hilltown, Wrexham in North Wales. Again like Davies his V.C. is in the possession of the R.W.F. Museum at Caernarfon Castle, Caernarfon.

Highland Memorial Park, Johnston, Rhode Island, USA (D. C. Jennings)

T. W. H. Veale

Pte. T. W. H. VEALE, V.C.

Gallahers Cigarette Card

attempts to capture the German Second Line, when they were called upon to help with the capture of High Wood on the 14th and again on the 20th. Their position was to the south west of the wood itself and their role was to attack towards Delville Wood in an easterly direction. At the time heavy fire was coming from the Switch Line at the northern edge of High Wood and also from the northern edge of Delville Wood.

The 8th Devons were part of the 20th Bde. of the 7th Division and they attacked with their sister battalion, the 2nd Gordons on their left.

The 8th Devons had already seen heavy fighting for the village of Mametz on July lst 1916 as well as being involved in the

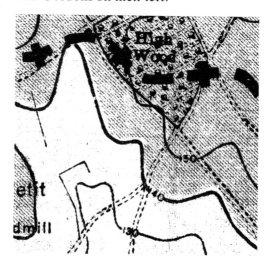

High Wood July 20th 1916

The immediate target of the two battalions was a track called Wood Lane which was a route that ran along the eastern side of High Wood and then in a south easterly direction. It was very heavily defended by the Germans. It was clear that the task of the 20th Bde. was bound to be a hopeless one until the whole of High Wood had been cleared which did not happen until two months had passed. During the fighting Pte. Theodore Veale had gone up to the front in order to assist the stretcher bearers and on hearing from a company corporal that someone was waving his hand to come in, he snatched up a rifle and bomb and went out for about 50 yards when several shots went by him. In his own words when writing to his mother about the incident

he wrote:

"I flopped down on the ground, but got up again and ran on till I got to the spot where the man had been waving. To my surprise it was one of our wounded officers (Lt. Eric Savill later Sir Eric) I laid down and did all I could for him, and I was well fired at whilst I was there. He (Savill) had been so close to the Germans, I pulled him back about 15 yards, for I found to my surprise that I was only about ten yards from the Germans. I pulled him back, thinking they were going to pull him in. I went back to get some water, and I took it out to him. They fired at me again, and it was surprising how it was that I was not hit. But I meant to save him at all costs; so off I crawled back again, because it was all open, and I got two more men and a corporal to come with a waterproof sheet, which we put him on.

We tried to pull him back. We got about 80 yards back, and then had to rest, for you know how one's back aches after stooping. Well, the corporal stood up like on his knees, and we saw five Germans pop up out of the grass about 100 yards away. We had to go over a bit of a bridge, and they shot the corporal (Cpl. Allen) through the head. That made the other two with me nervous, and they wanted to get back. So I said, "Get back, and I'll manage." So they went, and I pulled the wounded officer into a hole, and left him comfortable, and went back. Then I sent a team out to cover any of them that might try to fire at him, and tracked out to

Veale with his mother in the 1930s

30 and 32 Clarence Street, Dartmouth (B. Ward)

him myself with water." Later Veale went out with the Chaplain who was also acting as a stretcher bearer, Lt. Duff and Sergeant Smith. They reached Savill just before dark and just when they were going to get him home they spotted another group of Germans creeping up. Duff covered the Germans with his revolver while Veale risked his life and ran back for his gun a total of 150 yards and then raced back. At this fifth attempt Veale was able to drag Savill in with Lt. Duff's assistance.

The citation for Veale's V.C. was published in the *London Gazette* of September 9th 1916 and read as follows:

"For most conspicuous bravery. Hearing that a wounded officer was lying out in front, Private Veale went out in search, and found him lying amidst growing corn within fifty yards of the enemy. He dragged the officer to a shell hole, returned for water and took it out. Finding that single-handed he could not carry in the officer, he returned for assistance, and took out two volunteers. One of the party was killed when carrying the officer, and heavy fire necessitated leaving the officer in a shell hole.

At dusk Private Veale went out again with volunteers to bring in the officer. Whilst doing this an enemy patrol was observed approaching.

Private Veale at once went back and procured a Lewis gun, and with the fire of the gun he covered the party, and the officer was finally carried to safety.

The courage and determination displayed was of the highest order."

Pte. Veale did not receive his V.C. from the King at Buckingham Palace until February 5th 1917, and the first that he knew of his award was when he read about it in the Newspapers in the trenches.

———————

Theodore William Henry Veale was born in either 30 or 34 Clarence Street, Dartmouth, Devon on November 11th 1893. He was the eldest son of Henry Veale, a local builder and Ada Veale who was a professional concert pianist. The family address was 12 Mansard Terrace, Dartmouth.

Veale was educated at Dartmouth Council Schools and became a considerable athlete. At the beginning of the war when he was still only 20 years of age Veale was so impressed by the recruiting rallies that he went forward and became the first man in Dartmouth to volunteer.

With the Prince of Wales in 1921 (Dartmouth Illustrated)

At a film premiere in 1965 with A. Cross V.C. on the right

He joined the 8th Devons on September 4th 1914 and one of the men that he trained with at athletics was Lt. E. Savill.

After the award of the V.C. to Veale was announced there was considerable interest and excitement in the Devonshire town where Veale was a popular figure. When he returned home the town presented him with an Illuminated Address and an inscribed silver coffee service and salver. He had been promoted to the rank of Corporal on July 20th, the day that he gained the V.C.

One of the letters that Veale received was from Edwin Savill in which he thanked Veale for saving his son's life. Lt. Savill was to work for the Royal Family at Windsor Great Park after the war was over.

Three Devonshire men were to win the V.C. during the Great War and they rejoiced in the names of Veale, Sage and Onions. Sage served with the Somerset L. I. and the other two served with the Devonshire Regiment. In 1921 Veale was introduced to the then Prince of Wales who according to a press photograph is signing Veale's autograph book. Veale is apparently still in the Army as he is in uniform with his Corporal's stripes.

In 1966 he was one of a group of V.C. holders who were invited by the Ministry of Defence to take part in the 50th anniversary commemoration of the Battle of the Somme.

In 1968 Veale was employed as a Commissionaire at the Daily Mail Ideal Home Exhibition and became so hard up that he had to put his medals up for sale. They appeared in a shop window in Trafalgar Square in 1973 when Veale was living in Park Road, Balham, South London. Fortunately the Devonshire Regiment was informed and the asking price of £2,100 was raised and the medals are on display at the Devonshire and Dorset Regimental Museum at Exeter. In April 1980 with the aid of a walking frame Veale at the age of 87 reviewed a Passing Out Parade of Territorial Army Recruits of the Royal Engineers at Inglis Barracks, Mill Hill. He died on November 6th 1980 at his family home at Hoddesdon five days short of his 88th birthday. He was cremated on November 12th at Enfield after a full military funeral. He was one of the oldest surviving V.C. holders. His portrait hangs in the battalion officers' mess.

Sir Eric Savill the man who Veale rescued at High Wood died in April 1980 a few months before his rescuer.

Mr Theodore Veale, 87, who won the Victoria Cross for bravery in the Battle of the Somme in 1916, reviewing the Passing Out Parade of Territorial Army recruits in the Royal Engineers at Inglis Barracks, Mill Hill, yesterday. With him is the depot commandant, Col Rolph James. Mr Veale is believed to be the oldest surviving holder of the award, which he won while serving as a private in the Devonshire Regt.

Inglis Barracks, Mill Hill April 25th 1980

J. Leak

After the fighting for High Wood, Longueval and Delville Wood had not produced an Allied breakthrough the second phase of the Battle of the Somme began which was to include fierce fighting in and around the German held village of Pozieres. This village like the Gallipoli Peninsula was to be one of the places where the Australian nation was to 'finally come of age' in its sacrifice in men's lives, a price that it paid for its links with Great Britain.

Two V.C.s were to result from the fighting by the lst Australian Division on July 23rd 1916 and the first one by a matter of hours was won by Private John Leak of the 9th (Queensland) Bn. of the 3rd Bde. The British had reached the

German advanced position in front of Pozieres and the enemy lines ran in a south easterly direction from the direction of Mouquet farm, which in reality was just a ruined set of buildings. Before the Australian Division was called upon there had been three attempts to take the village all of which had failed.

The main defence lines were a double trench system known as O.G.1. and O.G.2. and on July 20th the 9th (Queensland) Bn. led the Australians into the area and an extremely fierce fight developed early on the 22nd. On the 23rd another attack was made with the lst Bde. on the left and the 3rd Bde. on the right. The 9th Bn. was covering 450 yards on the extreme right and under the shelter of

Gallahers Cigarette Card

later in the engagement they were driven back with Leak always the last to withdraw at each stage, covering his comrades' retreat. The post was retaken after reinforcements arrived. The fighting for the possession of Pozieres raged for four more days and the 9th Bn who had gone into battle with 1,016 men emerged with 623.

On August 21st Leak was wounded in the fighting at Mouquet Farm, near the village of Thiepval and 1500 yards north west of Pozieres. His V.C. was gazetted on September 9th 1916 and read as follows:

"For most conspicuous bravery. He was one of a party who finally captured an enemy strong point. At one assault, when the enemy's bombs were outranging ours, Private Leak jumped out of the trench, ran forward under heavy machine-gun fire at close range, and threw three bombs into the enemy's bombing post. He then jumped into the post and bayoneted three unwounded enemy bombers.

Later, when the enemy in overwhelming numbers was driving his party back,

a very heavy artillery barrage the troops made some progress. However at a point where O.G.l. met another trench called Pozieres Trench there was fierce German resistance and two machine guns held up the Australian units. The German bombs 'outranged' the Australian ones and it was at this point that Leak, without being given any instructions suddenly leapt out of his trench and ran forward and destroyed the enemy strongpoint and finished off the three survivors with the bayonet. When his comrades caught up with him they found him calmly wiping the German blood from his bayonet using his felt hat. The time was 12.59 a.m. Most of Pozieres Trench was taken but the 9th had nearly run out of bombs and

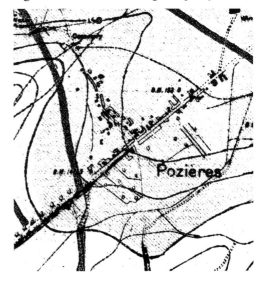

Pozieres July 23rd 1916

he was always the last to withdraw at each stage, and kept on throwing bombs. His courage and energy had such an effect on the enemy that, on arrival of reinforcements, the whole trench was recaptured."

He received his medal from the King at Buckingham Palace on November 4th 1916.

_____

John Leak was born in Portsmouth, England in 1892 and was half Welsh and half Australian; his father was James Leak, a miner. John Leak emigrated to Australia before the war started and became a teamster at Rockhampton, Queensland. On January 28th 1915 he enlisted with the A.I.F. and embarked on a troopship, joining the 9th Bn. at Gallipoli on June 22nd 1915. After the withdrawal from the Peninsula the

1st Australian Division arrived in France to take part in the fighting on the Somme.

After being wounded at Mouquet Farm in August 1916, Leak was out of action until he was fit enough to rejoin the 9th Bn. on October 15th 1917. On March 7th 1918 he was severely gassed at Hollebeke, Belgium and was unable to resume Army duties until June 26th. After the war was over in November 1918 Leak married Beatrice May Chapman at St. John Baptist, Cardiff, South Wales. In February he embarked for Australia and was demobilized from the A.I.F. in Queensland on May 31st. He remained in Queensland for two years before moving for two and a half years to New South Wales. He moved again to South Australia and then to the West. He married for a second time on January 19th 1927 Ada

J. Leak

Crafers in South Australia. In later years he suffered from bronchitis and emphysema which had been brought on by his war service and was unable to attend the Victoria Cross Centenary Celebrations in London in 1956. In 1966 a duplicate of Leak's V.C. turned up at a antique shop in Carlton, Victoria that the dealer said that he had purchased "years ago". Mr Leak said at the time that his V.C. had always been kept under lock and key but of course fakes were made of the medals from time to time. The Ministry of Defence thought it unlikely that two medals would have been struck for the same award. John Leak died on October 20th 1972 at the age of 80 and was survived by four sons and three daughters. He was buried at Stirling Cemetery. Adelaide and is commemorated at the Australian War Memorial in Canberra. His V.C. is in private hands.

Victoria Bood-Smith and by this time he had become a mechanic and a garage owner. When he retired he went to live at

A. S. Blackburn

Pte J. Leak gained his V.C. for gallantry at Pozieres Trench on July 23rd 1916 and the second Australian to gain the V.C on the same day was Lt. A. S. Blackburn. Four awards of the V.C. were to be awarded to the Australian units by the time that Pozieres was finally captured.

Within two hours of Pozieres Trench being captured the Australian Division were encountering very stiff enemy resistance at two lines called O.G.1 and O.G.2 which ran from the direction of Mouquet Farm in a south easterly direction and across the main Albert Bapaume road just south of the famous mill at Pozieres. The fighting resulted in the line being bent back at right angles. Less than a couple of hundred metres from the trench that had held up Pte. Leak's platoon the 10th (South Austra-

lian Bn.) of the 3rd Bde. of the 1st Australian Division was presented with a similar problem.

The 9th Bn. had already tried to attack O.G.1. from the south in order to subdue the German bombers and destroy the enemy machine gun. In the skirmish their commander Lt. Col W. F. J. McCann was seriously wounded in the head and their Adjutant Lt. C. H. Ruddle was killed. The Unit's source of bombs had dried up and they were driven down O.G.I. Trench to a point where they set up a barricade which was 120 yards short of Pozieres Trench. Reserve companies of the 10th Bn. under Major F. G. Giles then arrived from the south east (Black Watch Alley) in O.G.1. Seeing the situation Giles instructed Blackburn to take a party of 50 men along with two teams of battalion bombers, in order to continue the fight. At the barricade Blackburn found the remains of McCann's party who were exhausted. Blackburn with a small group from his own company together with a few bombers leapt over the barricade and rushed the Germans in order to bomb them out of their positions. Bay after bay were captured this way despite machine gun fire from O.G.2. and from the direction of Munster Alley which ran back at right angles from the German second line. Blackburn with a party of four men set off in order to destroy a troublesome enemy machine gun and in exposing themselves to German fire every one of the four men was killed. Blackburn returned for assistance and asked Colonel Robertson to arrange for Artillery cover and for trench mortar support. He then took another group of bombers and this time gained a further thirty yards.

The situation became very confused and the German resistance stiffened. Blackburn crawled forward with Sgt. R. M. Inwood and searched for the link between his 10th Bn. and the 9th. They found that there was a strong German position at a cross trench which cut O.G.I. at right angles. During the rush on this enemy post Inwood was killed and Blackburn's party was in danger of becoming cut off. They were saved by the finding of a tunnel which ran under the Pozieres-Bazentin Road and which by chance led to a group of men from the 9th Bn. in what was part of the eastern end of Pozieres Trench. Blackburn was sent out no fewer than four more times which meant eight times in all and howitzer protection was abandoned as it proved to be too unreliable. Blackburn had the assistance of seventy men of whom forty

had become casualties. Blackburn was finally relieved by a platoon under a Lt. Partridge who in turn was relieved and the attack towards the OG positions stopped 600 yards short of its goal. However Blackburn had been instrumental in providing the link up between the two battalions, the line was in fact broken but the two units had the gap covered. In this early fighting for the village of Pozieres the casualties were at their heaviest here and the Germans were at their most resolute.

It was hardly surprising that along with Pte. Leak, Lt. Blackburn was to be awarded the V.C. for all his hard work on this day and a miracle that he survived. The award was gazetted on September 9th 1916 and read as follows:

"For most conspicuous bravery, he was directed with fifty men to drive the enemy from a strong point. By dogged determination he eventually captured their trench after personally leading four separate parties of bombers against it, many of whom became casualties.

In face of fierce opposition he captured 250 yards of trench. Then, after crawling forward with a Sergeant to reconnoitre, he returned, attacked and seized another 120 yards of trench, establishing communications with the battalion on his left." He received the medal from the King at Buckingham Palace on October 4th 1916. He was the first man from South Australia to win the award.

———————

Arthur Seaforth Blackburn was born at Woodville, Hyde Park, Adelaide, South Australia on November 25th 1892. His father was Canon T. Blackburn who was rector of St. Margarets, Woodville for twenty years. His mother was Margaret Stewart formerly Browne and was the Canon's second wife. Arthur was edu-

Gallahers Cigarette Card

for Third Ridge." On August 4th he was promoted in the field to 2nd Lt and was still with 'A' Company but this time as platoon commander. In November the unit left the Peninsula for Lemnos and Egypt where he was made full Lieutenant on February 20th 1916. Before the Somme battle he was made platoon commander of 'D' Company. He was not well enough to continue as an active soldier and returned to Adelaide in December 1916. He married Rosa Ada second daughter of J. H. Kelly of Walkerville, and in time they were to have two sons and two daughters. He was discharged from the A.I.F. on April 10th 1917. He returned to the legal profession and became a member of the South

A. S. Blackburn April 1918

cated at St. Peter's College and the University of Adelaide where he graduated in 1913 and was called to the Bar in the same year at the age of 21. He lived at Hyde Park as a practising solicitor.

Fifteen days after the War began he was one of the first to enlist which he did with the 10th Bn. of the A.I.F. as a Private in Morphettville. He joined 'A' Company. We are told that he was not a 'sturdy youth'. They landed at Gallipoli on April 25th 1915 and with a friend Pte. P. Robin distinguished himself by reaching the furthest point after circling the east side of Scrubby Knoll, this was about 2000 yards from Anzac Cove. Robin was to be killed shortly afterwards. Their instructions had been "Go like Hell

Australian House of Assembly between 1918 and 1921. Four years later he entered into partnership with Lt. Col. McCann who had been with him at Pozieres and who had also been at the same medal ceremony at Buckingham Palace in 1916. They practised in Adelaide and Blackburn was appointed to the Reserve of Officers and served on various committees. He became city coroner in 1933 and in 1935 moved to 5 Salisbury Terrace, Collinswood.

By 1939 he had served as a militia officer for 15 years and was promoted to Lt. Colonel and took command of a motorised cavalry regiment. In 1940 he gave up the law and joined the 2nd/3rd Australian Machine Gun Battalion, A.I.F. which fought under his command in Syria in 1941. He and his group were later transferred to South East Asia and were forced by the Japanese to surrender in Java. He was liberated in Manchuria in September 1945 On his return to Adelaide he was greeted by three V.C. winners-T. Caldwell, P. Davey and Reg. Inwood. He was weak in health but not broken and in 1946 was given the C.B.E. (Military).

Between the years of 1947 and 1955 he served as conciliation commissioner in the Commonwealth Court of Conciliation and Arbitration. and took on various directorships. He died suddenly at Adelaide on November 24th 1960, one day short of his 68th birthday. He was buried with full military honours at West Terrace cemetery, Adelaide. He is commemorated at the Canberra War Memorial and his medals are in private hands.

T. Cooke

The third member of the Australian forces to gain the V.C. for gallantry at Pozieres was Pte. T. Cooke of the 8th Bn. of the 2nd Victorian Bde. of the 1st Australian Division. He was awarded it for action during the period July 24th/25th and not July 28th as several reference books tell us.

The Allies were still trying to complete their capture of Pozieres but had not succeeded in clearing the enemy out of the O. G. Trench positions. To quote C. E. W. Bean: "The right front company of the 8th, in pushing through Pozieres, met with heavy fire and the loss of three officers, but reached the post already held in the orchard, where a party of the 1st Pioneers at once began to dig a redoubt. . . . . but the intended positions between the village and the O. G. lines had not yet been occupied. . . . . At 8. 15, while the bombardment continued, large numbers of the enemy were seen advancing southwards on the crest near Pozieres windmill. This movement was observed from many parts of the Australian front, and was interpreted as an attempt to counter-attack." It was met by a heavy artillery barrage. Cooke had been ordered with his gun-team to a dangerous point, where he held out under heavy fire until all his comrades had been killed. When assistance was eventually sent he was found dead beside his gun. He was subsequently awarded the V.C. posthumously. His award was gazetted on September 9th 1916 and read as follows:

"For most conspicuous bravery after a Lewis gun had been disabled, he was ordered to take his gun and gun-team to a dangerous part of the line. Here he did fine work, but came under very heavy fire, with the result that he was the only man left. He still stuck to his post and

Pte. THOMAS COOKE. V.C.

Gallahers Cigarette Card

irresistible advance reached its objective by 5 a.m. and proceeded to establish itself 50 yards north of the cemetery. Our right company "C" met with strong .opposition, but fighting with great determination speedily overcame it, and shortly after 5 a.m., reached their objective N. E. of the village and at once dug in. Bombing parties of the 4th Bn. working up German Trench cooperated splendidly, driving the enemy towards positions occupied by our left company, where they were either killed or made prisoner." When the battalion was relieved two days later their total casualties were 347 with sixteen reported missing.

———

Thomas Cooke was the son of Tom and Caroline Ann Cooke and was born in Kaikoura, New Zealand on July 5th 1881 he was educated at Kaikoura Demonstration High School. He moved to Wellington as a young man and married Maud Elizabeth Elliott on June 4th 1902. In 1912 the family moved to Richmond, a suburb of Melbourne, Victoria and in time had three children. He was a builder by trade and his chief recreation was playing the cornet in a band. At the age of 33 he enlisted with the A.I.F. in Melbourne on February 16th 1915. and went with them to the Western Front. He was Acting Corporal from November 25th 1915 until February 24th 1916 when a member of the 7th Bn. but then relinquished his stripe when he transferred to the 8th Bn. After news of his posthumous award was published in New Zealand the inhabitants of his birthplace and in Wellington were delighted and an attempt to honour his memory was made but I have not found out what form it took.

Cooke's body was not retrieved but his name is listed on the Australian Memo-

continued to fire his gun. When assistance was sent he was found dead beside his gun. He set a splendid example of determination and devotion to duty."

The unit diary described the situation in the following way:

"At 3.30 under cover of artillery fire the attack was launched, the battalion attacking on a frontage of two companies "C" and "D" Coys.) right and left respectively with "B" Company in support. The attack proceeded vigorously through the village, and each trench and strong-point being quickly cleared of the enemy. The left company "D" with an

Pte. T. Cooke

81

Pozieres July 24th/25th 1916

rial at Villers-Bretonneux, where men are listed by rank alphabetically and in Regimental order. He is also commemorated at the Australian War Memorial at Canberra. His medals are in private hands.

Villiers Bretonneux Memorial (C.W.G.C.)

Villiers Bretonneux Memorial (D. C. Jennings)

A. Gill

Gallahers Cigarette Card

By July 25th the British had abandoned their series of attacks to capture High Wood which they were not to achieve until mid September. However the next day brought them the prize of the capture of Pozieres village which the Germans had been very loathe to let go. On the 28th the British were to finally capture the village of Longueval and the adjacent Delville Wood. This was not achieved without heavy fighting and the winning of

another posthumous award of the V.C. this time by Sergeant Albert Gill. His battalion was the lst K.R.R.C. of the 99th Bde of the 2nd Division. The other three battalions in this Bde. were the lst. R. Berks. and two units of the Royal Fusiliers the 22nd and 23rd Battalions.

At 7 a.m. on the 27th the 99th Bde made what was to be the final assault to clear the enemy from Delville Wood. The lst R. Berks, the lst K.R.R.C. and the 23rd R. Fus. led the attack and drove the Germans to the fringe of the wood. However there was a strong German counter-attack and it was during this period of fighting that Sgt. Gill was to gain his V.C. The citation was published on October 26th 1916 and read as follows:

"For most conspicuous bravery. The enemy made a very strong counter-attack on the right flank of the battalion, and rushed the bombing post after killing all the company bombers.

Sgt. Gill at once rallied the remnants of his platoon, none of whom were skilled

bombers, and reorganised his defences, a most difficult and dangerous task, the trench being very shallow and much damaged. Soon afterwards the enemy nearly surrounded his men by creeping up through the thick undergrowth, and commenced sniping at about twenty yards range. Although it was almost certain death, Sgt. Gill stood boldly up in order to direct the fire of his men. He was killed almost at once, but not before he had shown his men where the enemy were, and thus enabled them to hold up their advance.

A. Gill

Delville Wood July 27th 1916

For his supreme devotion to duty and self sacrifice he saved a very dangerous situation."

The wood was finally and completely cleared of the enemy by the 2nd Div. on the 28th.

―――――――

Albert Gill was the son of Henry and Sophia Gill and was born on September 8th 1879 at Hospital Street, Birmingham. The family later lived in Dugdale Street which has been redeveloped and later Gill himself was to live at 2 Back of Cope Street, Spring Hill, Birmingham. Before joining up he worked for the Post Office for 17 years and was about 35 years of age when the Great War began.

Three weeks after Gill was killed, his company commander wrote to Mrs Rosette Gill in a letter dated August 16th 1916: "The Adjutant has handed me your letter of the 8th of August, as I was your late husband's Company Commander. I am afraid that it is quite true that your husband was killed in action on July 27th. He was shot in the head, and must have died at once. He could have known nothing about it. I would have written to you before had I known your address, as

Delville Wood Cemetery (D. C. Jennings)

your husband was one of the most valued men in my company and who anyone would be proud to call friend. He was killed when rallying his men under terrible fire, and had he lived he would certainly have got the D.C.M. I was quite close to him, despite the very trying circumstances. The battalion had just taken a wood (Delville), and the Germans were counter-attacking heavily. I am glad to say we drove them back, and we have since received the thanks of everyone, from Sir Douglas Haig down. It was entirely owing to the heroic example and self-sacrifice of men like your husband that we did so well. He was loved by his platoon, of which I am sorry to say only four or five men remain. That day's work will always remain fixed in my memory as the one in which I lost so many gallant comrades. I lost all the officers and sergeants in my own company, and

Delville Wood Cemetery (C.W.G.C.)

very many of the men. You should be justly proud of your husband in his life and death. He had one of the finest natures I have ever known. No words of mine can express my sympathy with you in your terrible sorrow. May the memory of his heroic end support you."

Mrs Gill was presented with her husband's V.C. by the King at Buckingham Palace on November 29th 1916.

Gill was buried at Delville Wood cemetery Row IV, C, 3 and was the fourth man to gain the V.C. for the fight for Delville Wood. His medals were sold at Sothebys on July 19th 1965 for £800 and are in private hands.

C. C. Castleton

Gallahers Cigarette Card

The main part of the village of Pozieres had been captured by July 26th 1916 but the struggle for possession of the Pozieres Heights was not finally won by the Allies until August 4th. July 29th was to be the

day when the fourth member of the Australian Imperial Force was to gain the V.C. and like Pte. T. Cooke before him he was to lose his life in doing so. His name was Sgt. Claude Castleton of the 5th Australian Machine Gun Company. The Unit was part of the 2nd Australian Division which had replaced the 1st Australian Division and of the 5th (New South Wales Bde.). There were four battalions in the Bde. the 17th, 18th, 19th and 20th.

Before midnight on July 28/29th the Germans had seen leading troops of the 20th Battalion moving into assembly positions to the south of the Albert-Bapaume Road and had fired on the second wave of men with machine guns. This fire was accompanied by flares and a German barrage and the Australians had to lie out for three hours until the machine gun fire had subsided. Just before dawn the troops were withdrawn and the "makeshift" jumping off arrangements had led directly to this disaster. The leading wave of the 17th Bn. had also been detected by the enemy when they were climbing out of their trenches in order to bomb up the O.G.2. position. The bombing attack was called off because there was no sign of the 20th's attack. When the 20th Bn. had withdrawn, Castleton, who was stationed at the sand-bag block in O.G.1. went out

Pozieres July 28th 1916

Pozieres British Cemetery (D. C. Jennings)

into no man's land in order to rescue some of the wounded whom he had seen lying there. It was in the same vicinity where Lt. A. S. Blackburn and Pte. J. Leak had also won the V.C. Castleton brought in two men and was struck by a bullet and killed when bringing in a third casualty. His citation was published on September 26th 1916 and read as follows:

"For most conspicuous bravery. During an attack on the enemy's trenches the infantry was temporarily driven back by the intense machine gun fire opened by the enemy. Many wounded were left in "No Man's Land" lying in shell holes.

Sjt. Castleton went out twice in face of this intense fire and each time brought in a wounded man on his back.

He went out a third time and was bringing in another wounded man when he was himself hit in the back and killed instantly.

He set a splendid example of courage and self-sacrifice."

The 5th Bde. had lost 146 men including 6 officers, mostly from the 20th Bn. Castleton's body was eventually laid to rest in Pozieres British Cemetery, Row IV, L, 43. and his posthumous V.C. which was recommended by the Brigadier-General commanding the 5th Australian Bde. was presented to his father by the King at Buckingham Palace on November 29th 1916.

———————

Claude Charles Castleton was the son of Thomas Charles Castleton and his wife Edith Lucy Castleton and was born in Morton Road, Kirkley, South Lowestoft, Suffolk on April 12th, 1893. He was educated at Morton Road School and later at the local Grammar School. He was a very practical and adventurous boy and used to take himself off camping and sailing on the Norfolk Broads during the school holidays. Later he became a pupil teacher at Morton Road School where he had himself gone as a child and had won a scholarship. His father was a builder and the family house was at 18 Wilson Road which is adjacent to Morton Road.

At the age of 19 Castleton decided to emigrate to Australia with the idea of seeing as much of the world as he could, before settling down in England again. He worked on a sheep farm and tried his hand at prospecting gold. He moved on to Tasmania and then travelled extensively thoughout Victoria, New South Wales and Queensland. When war broke

Pozieres British Cemetery (C.W.G.C.)

South Cliff Congregational Church, South Lowestoft (W. Fullaway)

South Cliff Congregational Church, South Lowestoft (W. Fullaway)

out in August 1914 he was in Port Moresby, Papua, New Guinea. He offered his services and was with one other white man in charge of a large number of Aborigines who carried out coastal defence duties. Later he worked at a cable and wireless station before returning to Sydney where he enlisted in March 1915. He stated his occupation as prospector.

He sailed to the Gallipoli Peninsula with the Anzac Forces, as a member of the 18th Australian Battalion. During the action at Anzac Cove he was to show qualities of leadership and courage when on losing an officer and a sergeant the fellow members of his company turned to him as their natural leader. On leaving the Peninsula, Castleton was promoted to the rank of Corporal. On February 20th 1916 he was made a temporary sergeant and on March 8th was transferred to the 5th Machine Gun Company. He was confirmed as a sergeant on March 1916. Before going to France his Division served briefly in Egypt.

After Castleton was killed in July 1916 a comrade wrote to his father and said: "We were helping to hold a first line of trenches, when our infantrymen made an attack on the enemy. As may be expected, we had some casualties. Claude, knowing some of our wounded men to be out in 'No Man's Land', could not resist going to their assistance. Amidst shrapnel and heavy m.g. fire and gas, he leaped out, and recovered two wounded men, and was in the act of bringing in a third, when to our sorrow, he was either hit by rifle or m.g. fire. First aid men went to his assistance immediately, but could do no good; he had done his last. We gave him a decent burial behind our front line, erecting a small cross with his name, number etc, over his grave. His name will

18 Wilson Road, South Lowestoft (W. Fullaway)

stand forever amongst the officers and men of his company, and also with the infantrymen and officers to whom we were attached. . ."

After the war his parents paid for a

plaque to be put up in South Cliff United Reform Church, Morton Road which is where the family worshipped and is still in existence. The church itself is only about 90 years old. Castleton's name is also listed on an oak panel at St. Margarets Parish Church, Lowestoft. At one time a portrait of him hung in the Town Hall and his V.C. medal was still in the possession of the family in 1968 but has since been acquired by the Australian War Memorial in Canberra. Claude's brother Frank became Town Clerk of Folkestone, Kent and the small terraced house where the family lived, number 18 Wilson Street, South Lowestoft, still exists, although it has been completely 'modernised'.

W. J. G. Evans

Sgt. Evans with family at Buckingham Palace 1920 (TMB)

The 30th Division consisted of the 21st, the 89th and 90th. Brigades. In the last named brigade were three battalions of the Manchester Regiment, the 16th, 17th and 18th as well as the 2nd Royal Scots Fusiliers Battalion.

Earlier in July 1916 the Division had been involved in the capture of Montauban and Trônes Wood. It was later withdrawn in order to be made ready for an attack on the very strongly held village of Guillemont. The 21st Bde. had a go on the 23rd but was let down by a lack of artillery support. The second attempt to capture the village was planned to be made on July 30th, a day which began as very misty and then became very hot with temperatures in the 80s. The 30th Div. was to attack through the lines of the 35th Div. The 89th Bde. was to reach the southern end of the village and the 5th Bde. (2nd. Div) was to capture Guillemont Station and the enemy trenches beyond it. Zero hour was 4.45 a.m. and Maltz Horn Farm was quickly taken and the advance continued downhill in an easterly direction. The 18th Manchesters had left the assembly trenches at Brick Lane for the three mile walk to Guillemont via Trônes Wood and the enemy sensing an attack bombarded their route and used gas shells as well. Although men wore gas helmets they became stifled by them and also lost all sense of direction. Trônes Wood in addition was a nightmare of unburied bodies and smashed trees. The battalion emerged finally on the east side of the wood at 4.30 a.m. and they were due at their assembly positions at 5.00 a.m. The attack was carried out in a heavy ground mist and the 89th Bde. advanced on the right and the 90th on the left. The two leading battalions of the latter Bde. the 18th Manchesters and the

2nd Royal Scots reached their positions in the western part of the village but without the back-up of artillery. Worse was to follow in that the German artillery was so accurate that any support was cut off by it. The Royal Scots were virtually annihilated and the 18th and two companies of the 17th Manchesters were taken prisoner. It was during this chaos that Company Sergeant Major George Evans of 'B'Company (18th Manchesters) was to gain the V.C. and his citation, which was published on January 30th 1920 read as follows:

"For most conspicuous bravery and devotion to duty during the attack on Guillemont on 30th July, 1916, when under heavy rifle and machine gun fire he volunteered to take back an important message after five runners had been killed in attempting to do so. He had to cover about 700 yards, the whole of which was under observation from the enemy.

Company Serjeant-Major Evans, however, succeeded in delivering the message, and although wounded, rejoined his company, although advised to go to the dressing station.

The return journey to the company again meant a journey of 700 yards under severe rifle and machine gun fire, but by dodging from shell-hole to shell-hole he was able to do so, and was taken prisoner some hours later.

On previous occasions at Montauban and Trônes Wood this gallant Warrant Officer displayed great bravery and devotion to duty, and has always been a splendid example to his men."

'B' Company had been almost entirely

Sgt. Evans with family at Buckingham Palace 1920 (TMB)

made up of recruits from Lloyd's Packing House in Manchester and the total number of casualties of the 18th Manchesters for the attack against Guillemont was 476 including killed, wounded and missing. This figure included sixteen officers. As we have seen Evans himself was one of those taken prisoner.

Evans' V.C. was to be the last one gazetted in the Great War, the last of 634 to be awarded. He was given it in March 1920 and the reason for the delay was that he had been made Prisoner of War and probably those who recommended him for the award were also POWs.

———————

George Evans was born on February 16th 1876 in Kensington, West London. His father was Daniel Jones Evans and his mother was Georgina Evans who died when he was six weeks old. His father died when he was thirteen. He was educated at several schools and as a result became very self reliant. He also grew up a fairly burly man to a height of six feet. At the age of eighteen he joined the Scots Guards in March 1894 and served in the South African War between 1899 and

Sgt. Evans (TMB)

1902 with the 1st Battalion. He was for six months in Orange Free State. During the war he was a member of the Imperial Representative Corps which accompanied the Royal Family when they visited Australia for the Comonwealth Celebrations. He returned to South Africa and served in the final part of the Boer War. He became an Instructor for the Scots Guards but after eight years he was discharged in August 1902. He was then three years with the Derby Borough Police Force and later in Manchester he began a very successful career with the Children's Society, the NSPCC, as an Inspector. However a few months after war began in August 1914 Evans rejoined the Army on January 4th 1915. He did not join the Guards but the Manchester Regiment, (3rd City Pals), two months later he was promoted Second Class Warrant Officer, Company Sergeant-

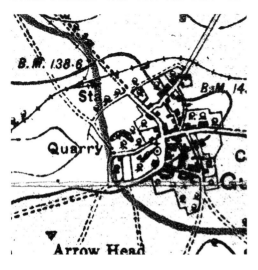

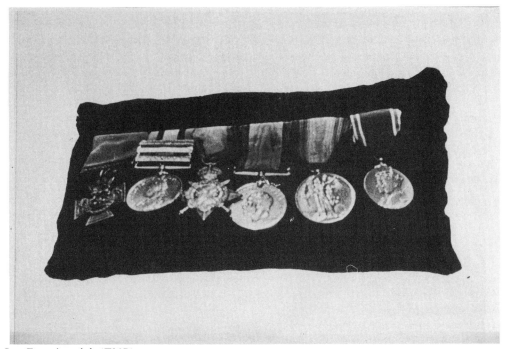

Sgt. Evans' medals (TMB)

Major on March 15th. He left for France on November 8th 1915 and was wounded in the arm during the Somme fighting before he was taken prisoner.

He was later to say that as a prisoner of war he was treated like a criminal and spent the two years in various German camps. He existed on parcels from home and lost six stone in weight. He was exchanged and arrived in Holland on June 6th 1918, but it was not until November 19th 1918 that he was sent back to England and finally demobilised on February 20th 1919. George Evans had married Clara Bates and they had four children, two boys and two girls. Clara deputised for her husband in the NSPCC when he was away between 1915 and 1920. Their first home was 62 Woodlands Road, Manchester. In 1920 Evans was presented with a wallet containing the proceeds collected from a

Sgt. Evans on the left, 1920s (TMB)

Elmers End 1937 (TMB)

Elmers End Cemetery, Beckenham 1937 (J. Boys)

public fund at the Higher Crump Constitutional Club, Manchester.

Evans who through his work with the NSPCC became known as the "Children's V.C.", returned to live and work in London, he was first stationed in Hackney and then in Sydenham, where he died suddenly at his home at 5 Tremaine Road, Annerly, South London, on September 28th 1937 at the age of 61. He was buried with full military honours at Elmers End Cemetery, Beckenham, which is close to Annerley. There was a bearer party from the Scots Guards in attendance and *The Last Post* and *Reveille* were played at the graveside. Evans's six medals were born on a cushion at the ceremony and Masonic Funeral Rites were observed. His funeral was a pretty grand affair and many local dignatories attended as well as colleagues from the Scots Guards, the Manchester Regiment and the NSPCC. A memorial service to his memory was also held in Manchester Cathedral. Evans' civilian grave is looked after by the local Scots Guards Association. His name was inscri-bed in the memorial in the Guards Chapel in Birdcage Walk, London as well as being listed in the memorial books of the Manchester and King's Regiments in Manchester Cathedral. His medals are in private hands.

J. Miller

On July 30th 1916 the principal III Corps operation was to try and capture the Intermediate Trench which was to the north of Bazentin le Petit and due west of High Wood. The Division to be involved was the 19th (Western) and the Brigade the 57th. This Brigade consisted of 10th R. Warwicks, 8th Glosters, 10th Worcs., and 8th N. Staffs. The 7th King's Own were also to be involved and they were attached from the 56th Bde. The British concentrated artillery fire on the north west part of High Wood and the Switch

Gallahers Cigarette Card

Bazentin le Petit July 31st 1916

Line which was to the north of the wood. The King's Own and and the 10th R. Warwicks closed right up to the barrage. The Intermediate Trench and the Germans in it were rushed, but owing to the slowness of the Worcesters and the Glosters in arriving, ground was lost as the German machine guns had recovered from the swiftness of the sudden attack. Part of the Intermediate Trench was retained with the help of the 5th South Wales Borderers and the 81st Field Company R. E. German shell fire made movement difficult and communication with the front line well nigh impossible. It was in this situation that Pte. John Miller was to gain a posthumous V.C.

Miller was ordered to take a message during a break in communications and his citation which was published on September 9th read as follows:

"For most conspicuous bravery. His battalion was consolidating a position after its capture by assault. Private Miller was ordered to take an important message under heavy shell and rifle fire and to bring back a reply at all costs.

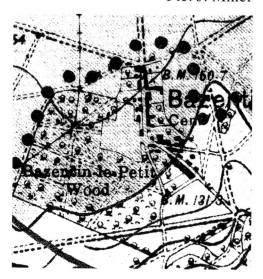

He was compelled to cross the open, and on leaving the trench was shot almost immediately in the back, the bullet coming out through his abdomen. In spite of this, with heroic courage and self-sacrifice, he compressed with his hand the gaping wound in his abdomen, delivered his message, staggered back with the answer, and fell at the feet of the officer to whom he delivered it.

He gave his life with a supreme devotion to duty."

He was buried at Dartmoor Cemetery near Bécordel, Plot l. Row C, Grave 64 and his medal was presented to his father by the King at Buckingham Palace on November 29th 1916.

Dartmoor Cemetery (D. C. Jennings)

James Miller was born at Taylor's Farm, Hoghton, near Preston on March 13th 1890. He was the son of George and Mary Miller. The family later moved to 1, Ollerton Terrace, Withnell near Chorley. Miller went to school at Abbey Village Primary School and went to work at a Wiggins Teape papermill at Withnell Fold. He was a popular local footballer.

On the outbreak of war when he was 24

Dartmoor Cemetery (C.W.G.C.)

also placed near to Miller's place of work at the Wiggins Teape papermill.

The secretary of the King's Own Old Comrades' Association wrote a poem that tells the story of Miller's gallantry which is called "The Message."

In 1988 it was decided to clean and restore the memorial at the church and an appeal was launched by the vicar on behalf of James Arnold, a nephew of James Miller. Mr Arnold was overwhelmed and with help from the Royal British Legion and others the memorial was restored and made ready for rededication in August 1988. The medal of the V.C., which is normally kept in a bank vault was included in the memorial

he enlisted with the 7th King's Own Royal Lancaster Regiment, one of the New Army units. The battalion was formed at Bowerham Barracks and left for France on July 18th 1915. Six of his brothers also joined the Colours, and two of them did not survive the war. Miller saw action at Lens and Loos in Autumn 1915 and his battalion moved to the Somme in April 1916. They were in action at La Boisselle between July 3rd and 7th and spent the end of July consolidating at Mametz Wood and then Bazentin le Petit.

A memorial was raised at Withnell by public subscription and unveiled by Lt. Col. Thorne of the King's Own on July 14th 1917. Medals were presented on the same occasion. The memorial took the form of a Celtic Cross and was erected on the edge of the village churchyard at St. Pauls, Withnell. A memorial stone was

St Paul's Withnell (J. M. Garwood)

procession as it was worn by Mr Arnold. The procession was organised by the Chorley branch of the Royal British Legion and there was a good turnout for the parade and service, and wreaths were laid. Mr Arnold owns his late uncle's shaving mirror which was twisted by the impact of a bullet. The V.C. Medal itself is now in the hands of the Regimental Museum at Lancaster.

W. H. Short

Gallahers Cigarette Card

Of the 51 V.C.s to be awarded for gallantry during the battle of the Somme 26 were won in July, a fact that reflects that most such awards are given for the period at the beginning of a major battle. Conversely only four were to be awarded for the fighting in the month of August which suggests that it was the quietest month of the whole battle. The first of these four was to be won in Munster Alley.

In the week since Private Miller won his posthumous award at Bazentin le Petit, the battle had raged mainly in and around the village of Pozieres. The German Second Line on a front of 2,000 yards to the north of the village had been taken, as had ground to the west and to the east towards the village of Martin-puich. The Germans had tried to re-take Delville Wood but had failed and the fight for Guillemont had also continued.

The 23rd Div. of III Corps made a new attempt to capture Munster Alley on the night of August 4th/5th 1916. This position was part of the German Trench system called O.G.2 and was on the south-east side of the Albert-Bapaume Road and ran back at right angles towards Martinpuich. The Allied equiva-

Munster Alley August 6th 1916

lent trench was opposite it and ran in a south-westerly direction, this trench was called Pozieres Trench. The 23rd Div., contained the 68th, 69th and 70th Bdes. The 69th had two battalions of the Green Howards in it, the 8th and 9th. The other two units were the 11 W. Yorks. and the 10 D.W.R. Before they attacked however the 68th Bde. gained 60 yards on Munster Alley but was not able to make progress over open ground towards Torr Trench.

On the afternoon of the 6th the 8th Green Howards managed to bomb the enemy out of 150 yards of Munster Alley and also gained part of the eastern end of Torr Trench. Although two Lewis guns were brought up to cover Munster Alley and Torr Trench, it was the divisional artillery who had really done the work in

that the guns virtually blew Torr Trench out of existence. The ground became unrecognizable and defences were totally destroyed and the German dead lay all around. It was during this engagement that Pte. William Short was to gain a posthumous V.C. Short was a company bomber and was seriously wounded in the foot but refused to go back for treatment. Later when his leg was shattered he still refused to withdraw and lay in the trench adjusting detonators and straightening pins for his bomber comrades. His battalion was relieved at 9 p.m. by part of the 11th. W. Yorks. after they had been bombing and attacking for five hours. Short who was the third member of the Green Howards to win the V.C. in the battle of the Somme died of his wounds the next day on August 7th, he was 29

Contalmaison Chateau Cemetery (D. C. Jennings)

years of age. His medal was presented to his father on November 29th 1916.

Short's citation was published on September 9th 1916 and read as follows:

"For most conspicuous bravery. He was foremost in the attack, bombing the enemy with great gallantry, when he was severely wounded in the foot. He was urged to go back, but refused and continued to throw bombs.

Later his leg was shattered by a shell, and he was unable to stand, so he lay in the trench adjusting detonators and straightening the pins of bombs for his comrades.

He died before he could be carried out of the trench. For the last eleven months he had always volunteered for dangerous enterprises, and has always set a magnificent example of bravery and devotion to duty."

William Short was the son of Mr James Short and Mrs Annie Short and was born

Contalmaison Chateau Cemetery (C.W.G.C.)

at 11, William Street, Eston, Middlesbor-
ough, Yorkshire on February 4th 1887.
Some records say that he was born in 1901
but this was the date of his baptism. As a
boy he continued to live in Eston and as a
young man he lived at 35 Vaughan Street,
Grangetown, Yorkshire. He was a popular local footballer and became known as
"Twiggie" Short. He played for Grangetown Albion, Saltburn and Lazenby
United Clubs. The only photograph of
him that seems to exist is one of him taken
in football kit. William had two brothers,
Harry and Enoch and one sister.

As a young man before the war Short
worked as a craneman at the steelworks
at Eston called Bolckow, Vaughan &
Co., he enlisted on September 2nd 1914
and served at the Front from August 26th
1915 until his death. Shortly before his
death he was given ten days special
furlough for gallantry in the Field.

After the war a memorial in the form of
an obelisk was built in Grangetown to
Short's memory and was unveiled by
Councillor W. G. Grace on July 26th
1919. Short's commanding officer who
had lost an arm during the war, Lt. Col.
B.C.M. Western was one of the official
guests at the unveiling ceremony. The
obelisk built of Cleveland ironstone was
in the Town Square at Grangetown but
was later moved to Eston Cemetery.

Grangetown Memorial July 1919

Short's mother died after the second
war and his father, sister and brother
lived on at 18 Leighton Road, Grangetown for a number of years.

G. G. Coury

The village of Guillemont had been
attacked at the end of July and a plan was
drawn up to attack it again on August 7th.
It was on the boundary of the XlII Corps
and the 55th Div. was the unit that was
going to bear the brunt of the fighting.
On the right the French Sixth Army was
going to attack at the same time.

The 55th Div. contained three briga-

des; the 164th, 165th and the 166th and
the attack against the positions in front of
Guillemont began at 4.20 a.m. On the
right the 165th Bde. made a little progress
before being stopped by fire to the south
of the village. On the left of the 165th
Bde. was the 164th and two of their
battalions the l/5th King's and the l/4th
King's Own were checked in front of the

REFERENCE.

Enemy original system of defence	
Our original front of attack	
Line reached and maintained 1st July	
Line reached in fighting between 2nd & 13th July	
Our second advance—14th July	
Line held—12th September	
„ „ 18th „	
„ „ 27th „	
„ „ 17th November	

Gallahers Cigarette Card

own life Major J. L. Swainson C.O. of the l/4th King's Own (164th Bde.), who unfortunately died of wounds soon afterwards. Swainson, originally of the Duke of Cornwall's Regiment was a holder of the D.S.O. For this action Coury was to be awarded the V.C., the place where the incident took place was Arrow Head Copse, very close to the German front line to the south west of Guillemont. Coury was a member of the 3rd battalion but was attached to, the l/4th South Lancs. the pioneer battalion of the 55th Division. Not only did he bring in Major Swainson under intense fire but he also re-organised his positions and subsequently defeated further German counter attacks. The battalion was to be in the region for three whole weeks before being relieved and sent to Aigneville for rest. Three days before he gained the V.C. Coury had quelled a panic in his company lines when he managed to have a trench fire extinguished. His citation was published on October 26th 1916 and read as follows:

"For most conspicuous bravery. During an advance he was in command of two platoons ordered to dig a communication

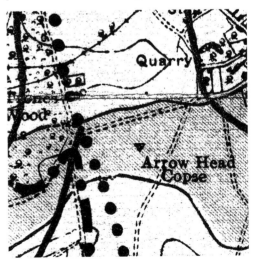

wire to the south west of Guillemont, and after trying to dig in beyond bombing distance of the Germans were forced to retreat to their assembly trenches. The l/8th King's also of the 164th Bde. broke through into the village but the l/4th Loyal N. Lancs. who were sent forward to hold the captured line were bombed out of it during a German counter attack.

2nd Lt. G. G. Coury was in charge of a Pioneer half company who were ordered to dig a forward communication trench, and he also attempted to rally the retreating troops when they were under very heavy fire. At the same time he was able to rescue, at great personal risk to his

Arrowhead Copse August 8th 1916

trench from the old firing line to the position won. By his fine example and utter contempt of danger he kept up his task under intense fire.

Later, after his battalion had suffered severe casualties and the Commanding Officer had been wounded, he went out in front of the advanced position in broad daylight and in full view of the enemy found his Commanding Officer, and brought him back to the new advanced trench over ground swept by machine gun fire.

He not only carried out his original tasks and saved his Commanding Officer, but also assisted in rallying the attacking troops when they were shaken and in leading them forward." Coury collected his V.C. from the King at Buckingham Palace on November 18th 1916.

———————

Gabriel George Coury was the second of four boys born to Raphael Coury, who was an Armenian and Marie Coury who was French. There were also two daughters. Gabriel was born at 16 Croxteth Grove, Sefton Park Road, Toxteth, Liverpool on June 13th 1896. He went to school first at St Francis Xavier's School, Salisbury, Liverpool and then to Stonyhurst College where he won many prizes for sports, and developed long and powerful arms and was well able to defend himself! He was at Stonyhurst which is in the Ribble Valley of East Lancashire from May 1907 until 1913.

His father had business connections with the cotton trade and Gabriel became an apprentice to the cotton firm of Reynolds and Gibsons (Brokers and Merchants.) in 1913. He enlisted in August 1914 at the age of 18 with the 6th

(Service) Bn. of the King's Liverpool as a Private. He carried out his training at Blackpool, Canterbury and Margate before receiving a commission with the 3rd Btn. in April 1915 but transferred to the 4th South. Lancs. in 1915. In October of that year the l/4th South Lancs. became a Pioneer Battalion and in January Coury joined with the Pioneers of the 55th (West Lancashire) Div. The Divison played no part in the early part of the Somme battle but at the end of July was in the Guillemont Region.

An eye witness, a Corporal from the South Lancashire Regiment, told of how Coury won his V.C. in the *Liverpool Post* of October 30th, 1916.

"He was the bravest officer I ever served under," . . . "The task given to the men under him was no soft one. To dig a new trench in the thick of a battle is a thing that requires some nerve, and a better officer than Lt. Coury could not have been chosen to direct the operation. He showed absolute contempt for death, and made us all feel that a dozen deaths were as nothing compared with the necessity of completing the task given to us. It was when we got into the captured position that Lt. Coury showed what he was capable of. We had gone through a hellish ordeal. We had suffered severely, and a lot of our officers and men lay out there in the open, wounded. It blew hurricanes of fire across the open, and it seemed to invite certain death to go out there. Word was brought that our commanding officer was among the wounded. Lt. Coury determined to go out to him. He started out under fiendish fire. The enemy's snipers were after him from the first, but he ran on regardless of the hail of bullets flying around him. He reached the spot where our commander lay, and after resting for a while started

G. G. Coury

back again, carrying the commander. The journey back was one of the most thrilling sights I have ever seen. The enemy redoubled their efforts to pick off the brave officer as he toiled painfuly towards our trench. Both he and his burden disappeared out of view for a short time, and we thought he was done for. After a time he appeared again, making his way amidst a storn of bullets and bursting shells. There was intense excitement, and we waited with baited breath, praying that he might be spared, but fearing the worst. The brave officer toiled slowly forward. Several times he stumbled, and we gave him up for lost. Once he fell. We thought he would never rise again; but rise he did, and resumed the terrible journey. Before he got back the enemy's machine guns were turned on full-blast and it was nothing short of a miracle that the Lieutenant was able to make his way through it all. At last he got within a few yards of our trench. We rushed out to meet him. He stumbled again, but regained his footing and continued straight on. Then there was another furious gust of fire. Down he went again. Would he ever rise, . . . Under heavy fire all the time, rescuer and rescued were helped into the trench, which was now being subjected to very severe artillery fire. Then the enemy tried a counter attack, and it was the duty of Lt. Coury to organise the defence. That he did with wonderful skill. He got together the men of different units and thoroughly organised the position. When the enemy tried to attack they were thrown back in confusion, and the counter attack was pressed home. The men were very enthusiastic over the capable way the situation had been handled when it was most difficult, and all were loud in their praise of our Lieutenant. Undoubtably he saved the day at its most critical stage."

On August 8th 1916 Coury was made a full Lieutenant and shortly afterwards joined the Royal Flying Corps in France as an Observer. When he attended his investiture in November 1916 he was in the uniform of the R.F.C. and shortly afterwards returned to Liverpool where he was given a very enthusiastic welcome. He was received by the Lord Mayor and given the Freedom of the Cotton Ex-

"Cora Lino", Merton Grove, Bootle, Lancs

change, the highest honour in the trade. In December he was also welcomed at St Francis Xavier's College when he returned to his old school. Two months later in February 1917 he visited Stonyhurst College and I was given a great reception. The College OTC provided a Guard of Honour. In November 1917 he was abroad ferrying an aircraft on its way when it crashed before reaching the channel, he was severely injured but recovered in hospital in Woolwich

On January 7th 1918 Coury married Katherine Mary Lovell at St. Mary's Church, Clapham and a daughter was born to the couple at the end of the year, and they were to have two more girls. In September he was made a Captain. He was one of seven members of Stonyhurst to gain the V.C.

After the war was over Coury returned to work for Reynolds & Gibson until 1926. He lived with his family at 2, Merton Grove, Bootle. In 1927 he moved to 38 Brooke Road, Waterloo. However he went with his wife to Alexandria, Egypt in about 1927 as a cotton shipper and agent. In 1940 he enlisted with the R.A.S.C. and in June 1944 took part in the Normandy Landings. He continued in the Army as the Allies advanced through France, Holland, Belgium and into Germany. When he returned from the war to his home in Liverpool he found

the cotton trade had virtually collapsed and that subsequently he was without work. He made a very brave decision and decided to open a fish and chip shop at 113 Brunswick Road, Liverpool. It was called 'The Frying Pan' and prospered. Coury was encouraged enough to open other food orientated businesses in the City. In 1954 the Liverpool Cotton Exchange reopened and Coury took a job with George H. Way as a manager and senior salesman. He left his other businesses in the hands of his wife.

In 1955 Coury's health broke down and he was admitted into Walton Hospital. He very nearly died and received the last sacraments. However he seemingly recovered and was discharged from hospital only to die at home on February 23rd 1956 age 59. He left a wife and three married daughters. His funeral took place at St. Peter and St. Paul, Great Crosby, Liverpool on February 26th, he was given full military honours and 300 people attended including a Boer War V.C. winner, Lt. Col. Donald Farmer. The South Lancashire Regiment sent a bearer party of National Servicemen.

On November 12th 1961 Coury's widow presented his V.C. to the Regiment at Warrington and in 1982 a replica of it which was on display in the Regimental Museum was stolen.

N. G. Chavasse

A fresh attack on Guillemont was planned for August 9th but owing to the British trenches to the forward of Trônes Wood being very congested it was difficult to get an attack going. The 164th Bde. (55th Div.) were ordered up when darkness fell the night before and then the XIII Corps insisted on a further effort

being made at 4.20 a.m. the next morning (August 9th).

Very little was accomplished during the night and not all the battalions were ready in position at zero hour. The initial bombardment was too hurried and the enemy was ready with very heavy machine gun fire. On the left the 166th

Gallahers Cigarette Card

devotion to duty.

During an attack he tended the wounded in the open all day, under heavy fire, frequently in view of the enemy. During the ensuing night he searched for wounded on the ground in front of the enemy's lines for four hours.

Next day he took one stretcher-bearer to the advanced trenches, and under heavy shell fire carried an urgent case for 500 yards into safety, being wounded in the side by a shell splinter during the journey. The same night he took up a party of twenty volunteers, rescued three wounded men from a shell hole twenty-five yards from the enemy's trench, buried the bodies of two Officers, and collected many identity discs, although fired on by bombs and machine guns.

Altogether he saved the lives of some twenty badly wounded men, besides the ordinary cases which passed through his hands. His courage and self-sacrifice were beyond praise."

Noel Chavasse was presented with his first V.C. by the King at Buckingham Palace on February 5th 1917.

Bde. was replacing the 164th Bde. at a difficult moment and there was resulting confusion. The l/10th King's (Liverpool Scottish) kept close up to the barrage but lost many men on getting near to the German wire. Many of the officers were hit and it was during this period that Captain Noel Chavasse of R.A.M.C. who was attached to The King's began his sterling work in saving the lives of his comrades. This heroism was to earn him the first of two Victoria Crosses and the second of five such awards to be given for the fight for Guillemont.

Chavasse's citation was published on October 26th 1916 and read as follows:

"For most conspicuous bravery and

Noel Godfrey Chavasse and his twin brother Christopher Maude were born on November 9th 1884 at the vicarage at St. Peter le Bailey, Oxford. Their father was the Reverend Francis Chavasse and their mother was Edith Jane Chavasse, who was a daughter of Canon Maude, Rector of Chirk. Noel was educated at Magdalen College School between the ages of 12 and 16. When his father was offered the post of the Bishop of Liverpool in 1900 the family moved up to Lancashire and lived in the Bishops Palace, which is now part of Liverpool University. Noel continued his education at Liverpool College School until the age of 20, when he left for

Trinity College, Oxford, where he remained for four years until 1908. He managed to get a First in physiology and won his University Blue in two sports. And both he and his brother were very good athletes but were not quite good enough to perform for their country. Noel was able to turn in a time of 10½ seconds for the 100 yards in 1907 when running in the inter varsity athletics. Noel began training for a medical career and when back in Liverpool after Oxford carried on with clinical studies. At the time he lived at home and carried out a great deal of 'muscular christianity' work in such places as boys clubs and reformatories. He did not fully qualify as a Doctor until 1912 when he was 27 and then took up the post of house physician at the Royal Southern Hospital, Liverpool and

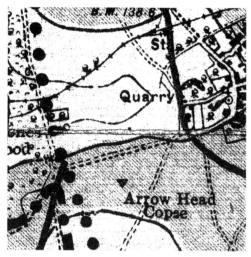

later he became house surgeon. This experience of course was to stand him in good stead a couple of years later. In 1913 he joined the R.A.M.C. and was

Guillemont August 9th 1916

attached to the 10th King's (Liverpool Scottish) and served with them in France and Belgium, having arrived in France as early as November 1914. Their first positions were in trenches in Kemmel at the time of the first battle of Ypres. In June 1915 the Liverpool Scottish saw action at Hooge near Ypres. This is where Chavasse first came to the notice of the military authorities in that he personally went out into no man's land for almost 48 hours until he was satisfied that no more wounded men were needing to be brought in. For this work he was awarded the M.C. The battalion was shattered and only gradually made up again in numbers with reserves from England. He asked one of his sisters to send a thousand pair of socks and other comforts at his own expense for the use of the men in his battalion.

On July 27th 1916 the battalion was moved into trenches in front of Guillemont and before their attack at 4.20 a.m. on August 9th had been unable to reconnoitre the positions. There was no British barrage during the previous night which allowed the enemy to repair his defences and to prepare for the expected attack. The supporting barrage began at 4.15 a.m., five minutes before zero hour. The battalion's total number of casualties were 189 men out of the 600 that the battalion had begun with.

Two months later the battalion had been made up to strength and found itself back in the Ypres Salient again. They carried on with routine trench duties and were in and out of the line for eight day periods. On July 20th 1917 they took over familar trenches near Wieltje, to the north east of Ypres and St Jean Preparations were being made for what was to become the third battle of Ypres, the attempt to capture the Passchendaele Ridge. The enemy was using mustard gas as a counter-barrage and the Liverpool Scottish were poorly protected against it. They lost 2 officers and 141 other ranks.

The British moved forward on July 31st, the first day of the new offensive, it was a dry and fair day. They made some progress into German held territory and captured some support trenches. In the evening Noel was wounded in the skull and was bandaged up but he refused to be evacuated. He kept close to his dressing station at Bossaert Farm. He continued to go out and collect and treat the wounded. There was very little food available and it began to rain which quickly turned the ground into a muddy swamp. In the early hours of August 2nd Noel was resting at his Aid Post when a

N. G. Chavasse Liverpool Scottish

Brandhoek New Military Cemetery, Belgium   (C.W.G.C.)

shell hit it. Everyone in the post was either killed or wounded including himself. Chavasse thought it unlikely that they would be given any help very quickly and despite having at least six wounds himself he set off for help and crawled half a mile for aid. He was then taken through Ypres to the 46th Field Ambulance at Brandhoek where he was examined by an American doctor, Dr. J. A. C. Colston.

Colston sent Chavasse on to the 32nd Casualty Clearing Station which was also in Brandhoek, his face was unrecognisable as it had been blackened by the shell burst. His abdomen was operated on and his other wounds were dressed. However his life could not be saved and after taking Holy Communion he died at around two o'clock in the afternoon of August 4th. Chavasse's battalion came out of the line

on the 3rd also to Brandhoek. Although they were tired and exhausted they insisted on attending their medical officer's funeral before getting any rest. They were once again sadly depleted in numbers. On his deathbed Chavasse dictated a letter to his fiancée, Gladys Chavasse who was a cousin. They had become engaged in April 1916. Her home was in Bromsgrove, Worcestershire. Some accounts say that she was in the Salient at the time with a special marriage licence which would have allowed the couple to marry anywhere, but it seems a hardly credible story. Of course she was unaware that Chavasse was seriously wounded and the letter to Gladys explained what had happened to him and why he had carried on with his work in the field despite having a fractured skull. Of his impending death he remarked to her "that duty called and duty must be obeyed".

For his work in the salient he was given a bar to his V.C. which of course was awarded posthumously, the only time that one man won two such awards in the Great War. The V.C. was presented to the next of kin. The citation was published on September 14th and read as follows:

"For most conspicuous gallantry and undaunted devotion to duty in action in front of Wieltje between July 31st and August 2nd 1917. Early in the action he was severely wounded in the head while carrying a wounded man to his dressing station. He refused to leave his post and for two days not only continued to attend to the cases brought to his first aid post, but repeatedly and under heavy fire went out to the firing line with stretcher parties to search for wounded and dressed those lying out.

During these searches he found a number of badly wounded men in the open and assisted to carry them in over heavy and difficult ground.

He was practically without food during this period, worn with fatigue and faint with his wounds.

By his extraordinary energy and inspiring example he was instrumental in succouring many men who must otherwise have succumbed under the bad weather conditions.

On the morning of August 2nd he was again wounded seriously by a shell and died in hospital on August 4th."

Noel Chavasse died only a few weeks after his brother Aidan had been reported missing and at the same time Noel's twin Christopher was serving as an Army Chaplain; he had lost a leg before the war and had to put up with the resulting pain for the rest of his life. He

was to be Bishop of Rochester for 21 years.

The wooden cross on Noel's first grave was sent home later to the Chapel of St. Peter's Oxford.

On October 8th 1917 Noel's kit arrived at his parent's home in Liverpool. He had left about £750 in his will to his brother Christopher who commissioned a portrait of Noel to give to his father as a birthday present. Noel's belongings were destroyed in the London Blitz, more than twenty years later.

A memorial service to the memory of the men who had lost their lives when serving with the King's (Liverpool) Regiment was held at St. Nicholas Church, Liverpool and the crowded congregation was made up of local

Brandhoek New Military Cemetery, Belgium (D. C. Jennings)

dignatories, members of the Regiment and of the relatives of the men. The north side of the church was occupied by the wives and relatives of dead soldiers. The Bishop of Liverpool was there as well as the Lord Mayor. The address was given by Archdeacon Spooner who alluded to Noel Chavasse and said "it was no wonder that the King felt that the whole Army would mourn the death of so brave and distinguished a brother, . . ." Gladys who had already been under pressure from her father not to marry Noel was naturally heart broken and was bitter that Noel had gone on caring for the wounded knowing that his own life would be threatened by the resulting exhaustion. Later Gladys used to record Noel's death every year in *The Times,* she also used to visit his grave at Brandhoek very regularly; the grave number is III, B, 15. Despite her devotion to Noel and his memory she did marry happily and lived until September 1962 when she was knocked down by a car when on holiday in France.

Christopher and Noel were one set of twins and they had twin sisters and there were three other children. Of these seven, five served in the War, and three won the M.C., and May one of the twin sisters who was a nurse at Etaples was Mentioned in Despatches. Dr. Bernard Chavasse, one of the brothers and a surgeon was killed in a car accident in 1942 .

The Chavasse medals were originally displayed on the staircase at St. Peters College, Oxford, but the insurers became nervous and replicas were made to replace the originals which were then locked away in a bank vault for about 15 years. The medals had been given to the College by Christopher in the 1930s. In 1979 the medals were allowed out of Oxford for a short while, for display at

the dedication of a memorial plaque at the headquarters of the Territorial Army Company of the Liverpool Scottish at Forbes House, Score Lane, Liverpool. Later St. Peters College and the Chavasse family decided that it might be a better idea to present the medals to the Imperial War Museum which they did on February 22nd 1990. Other Chavasse medals were lent but not given to the same museum (which had belonged to Bernard), and another group which had belonged to May one of the twin sisters who had served as a British Red Cross Nurse in the Great War and as a Queen Alexandra Nurse in the Second World War. May and her sister Marjorie, celebrated their 100th birthday in 1986 but have both died since. The Liverpool Scottish Museum had hoped to be given the Noel Chavasse medals and were disappointed when they weren't, as the Chavasse family was such a well known one in Liverpool.

At the time of writing there are at least 12 memorials to the memory of Noel Chavasse, more than for any other Somme V.C. holder and probably more than for any other V.C. anywhere in the world.

A plaque formerly in the Wellington Barracks. Liverpool was re-erected in the T.A. Centre and unveiled in October 1979. Mr Sam Moulton, Noel's former groom was present at the ceremony. Other memorials are at Trinity College, Oxford; Liverpool School, Liverpool Cathedral (Roll of Honour) and a memorial window, Liverpool Town Hall (Roll of Honour), Liverpool Cricket Club, Liverpool Scottish Memorial Board, Chavasse Park, Liverpool, a new office block named Chavasse House which has a mural inside and also two or three others.

M. O'Meara

Gallahers Cigarette Card

On August 10th 1916 General Gough issued orders for the Anzacs to have as their objective the enemy front positions which ran across the O.G. Trench lines, and thence south of a small quarry near the Pozieres-Thiepval road. The 12th Division was to capture Skyline Trench and the enemy line opposite the Nab, where the left of the 49th Div. would also attack. This plan was slightly altered in that west of Skyline Trench the Allies were only to carry out "holding attacks".

Major General Cox however wanted to see what his Anzac Troops could do first and was given permission. At 1 o'clock on the morning of the 11th after the usual preliminary bombardment two battalions of the Australian 4th Bde. of their 4th Div., the 13th (N.S.W.) and the 16th (S. & W. Aust) moved forward from Park Lane. The 13th established a frontal post to the south east of Mouquet Farm. The farm was to the north west of Pozieres and roughly between the villages of Thiepval and Courcelette. At dawn they held off a German bombing attack. On their left the 16th established themselves facing the quarry on the opposite slope. During the next twenty four hours the Germans attacked from the direction of Mouquet Farm and their artillery blasted the Australian forward positions. It was during this intense fighting that Pte. M. O'Meara (16th Bn.) was to gain the V.C. Later on August 12th the 16th Bn. were relieved by the 50th (S.A.) Bn.

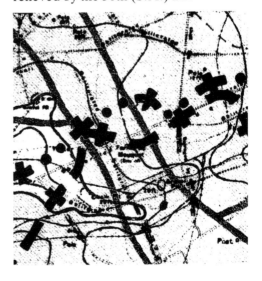

Pozieres August 9th to 12th 1916

The 16th Bn. had suffered very heavily during the continuous bombardment and fight and it was very difficult to reach their extremely exposed positions. However owing to the heroism of O'Meara the carriage of water, food and ammunition was sustained. He went through the artillery barrage four times and on one occasion took with him a party of men in order to bring out the battalion wounded. O'Meara did not rest until he was absolutely sure that all the wounded had been brought in. The 16th Bn. War Diary said that 'the trench as a trench had ceased to exist'. O'Meara was said to have rescued more than 25 men lying out in no man's land in conditions that were indescribable. The battalion had 406 casualties in four days.

O'Meara's V.C. citation was published on September 9th 1916 and reads as follows:

"For most conspicuous bravery. During four days of very heavy fighting he repeatedly went out and brought in wounded officers and men from "No Man's Land" under intense artillery and machine gun fire.

He also volunteered and carried up ammunition and bombs through a heavy barrage to a portion of the trenches, which was being heavily shelled at the time.

He showed throughout an utter contempt of danger, and undoubtedly saved many lives."

O'Meara was presented with his medal by the King on July 21st 1917.

Martin O'Meara was the son of Michael O'Meara who was a labourer and of Margaret O'Meara (formerly Connors) , and was born on November 6th 1885. His

M. O'Meara

O'Meara's V.C. (West Australian July 5th 1986)

place of birth was Lorrha, Rathcabbin, near Birr, County Tipperary, Ireland. As a young man he decided to emigrate and worked his passage to Australia as a ship's stoker.

He lived initially in South Australia before moving to the Western State where he enlisted with the A.I.F. in Perth on August 19th 1915 when he was nearly 30 years of age. He was 5 foot 7 inches and a Catholic and gave his occupation as a sleeper-hewer on the railways. Like so many Australian soldiers in the Great War he carried out his early training at Blackboy Camp, near Northam. He left Australia in December 1915 as one of a party of reinforcements for the 16th Bn. They trained in Egypt for a short time before leaving for France and the Western Front. As we have seen the 16th Bn. were involved in an attack on German positions to the north west of Pozieres close to Mouquet Farm.

After his exploits between August 9th and 12th 1916 he was first promoted Corporal on August 13th 1918 and then Sergeant on August 30th 1918. He was wounded three times; on August 12th 1916, April 9th 1917, and on August 8th 1917. In 1917 he managed to visit his native home in Ireland, and money was collected in the Lorrha region as a testimonial for the former resident. In his will dated 1917 he left the money collected for him to be spent on the restoration of Lorrha Abbey but it was not sufficient and instead the money was used for repairing the original parish church. O'Meara was a Roman Catholic, and had a sister in Ireland. He never married.

He served with the 16th Bn. for the rest of the war and was discharged from the A.I.F. in Perth on November 30th 1919. The rest of his life was spent in tragic circumstances as the experiences that he had in the war led to a complete collapse of his health. As a result he had to spend his remaining years in Military Hospitals. His illness was described as "chronic mania". He died 17 years after the war finished at Claremont Mental Hospital, Perth on December 20th 1935. His occupation listed on his death certificate was given as "returned soldier". He was buried in the Karrakatta Catholic Cemetery in Perth with full military honours, and his funeral was attended by three other holders of the V.C. His name is listed on the Australian War Memorial at Canberra. As he had no living relatives in Australia his medal was given to the 16th Bn. who in turn presented it to the Western Australian Museum in 1986.

W. B. Allen

Capt. W. B. ALLEN, V.C.

Gallahers Cigarette Card

No V.C.s were awarded during the period after August 12th 1916 until September 3rd, and this was because there had been little progress in the battle. Munster Alley near Pozieres was captured and the advance to the north west of Pozieres had been continued. However the German stronghold village of Guillemont was about to fall into Allied hands, and another operation was planned to take place to the north west of Guillemont astride the River Ancre; the history books describe it as 'The Ancre Attack.' The 49th Division on the right and the 39th Division on the left were to attack the German held ground from in front of the Redan Ridge south eastwards to the front of Schwaben Redoubt. The British artillery carried out a frontal bombardment but the two Divisions were unable to get a real foothold in the German positions. Indeed the enemy was

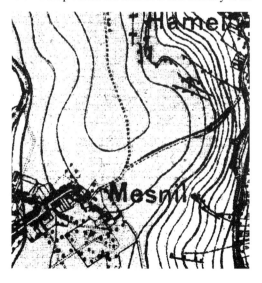

Mesnil September 3rd 1916

able to enfilade any trenches that he had lost temporarily, from the direction of St Pierre Divion. The Schwaben Redoubt too was virtually an impossible objective to take.

A battery of the CCXLVI. Bde. of the R.F.A. (49th Div.) was one of the units in action to the south west of Hamel, close to Mesnil, and was shelled with the result of many casualties. Captain W. B. Allen of the R.A.M.C. who was attached to the l/3rd West Riding (No 21) Field Ambulance 246th (W. Riding) Bde Territorial Force of the R.F.A. attended to the wounded with no regard to his own safety and was wounded several times in the process. His citation was published on October 26th 1916 and read as follows:

"For most conspicuous bravery and devotion to duty.

When gun detachments were unloading H.E. ammunition from wagons which had just come up, the enemy suddenly began to shell the battery position. The first shell fell on one of the limbers, exploded the ammunition and caused several casualties.

Captain Allen saw the occurrence and at once, with utter disregard of danger, ran straight across the open, under heavy shell fire, commenced dressing the wounded, and undoubtedly by his promptness saved many of them from bleeding to death.

He was himself hit four times during the first hour by pieces of shells, one of which fractured two of his ribs, but he never even mentioned this at the time, and coolly went on with his work till the last man was dressed and safely removed.

W. B. Allen in 1915

He then went over to another battery and tended a wounded officer. It was only when this was done that he returned to his dug-out and reported his own injury."

Allen was decorated by the King at Hyde Park on June 2nd 1917.

___

William Barnsley Allen was the son of Mr Percy E. Allen and Edith Barnsley Allen and was born in Sheffield on June 8th 1892. His parents home however was 6 Victoria Avenue, Scarborough, Yorkshire. William Allen's father was a salesman and sent his son to school at St. Cuthbert's College, Worksop. From there he went to the Sheffield Medical School in 1908, and joined the medical staff of the Royal Hospital at Sheffield in June 1914 at the age of 22. He had graduated with an M.B. and Ch.B. with Second Class Honours, a brilliant medical career lay in front of him but the start of war in August 1914 changed all that.

He enlisted on August 8th and was attached to the West Riding Field Ambulance and commissioned as a Lieutenant. He went to France in April 1915 and was made a Captain in the same month. In August 1916, he gained the M.C., in September the V.C. as we have seen, and in July 1917 he was awarded the bar to his M.C. He was invalided home on July 22nd 1917 for several months and on January 4th 1918 was made up to Acting Major. Three weeks before the Armistice he was wounded for the third time and again sent home sick to England. He was awarded the D.S.O. He was transferred to the Regular R.A.M.C. with the rank of Captain having finished the war as a Major. During the war he had been bayoneted in the side when helping the enemy wounded and on other occasions he received severe chest wounds, was gassed at another time and was blinded for six months.

After the war he went to India and was appointed to the staff of the Prince of Wales and the Duke of Connaught. However he was still very weakened by his war wounds and while in India contracted malaria and dysentry. He returned to England with his health completely broken. In 1924 he was attacked by sleepy sickness which was treated without success. In order to try and improve his health he moved to Bracklesham Bay on the south coast near Chichester, where he lived in a house in Stocks Lane called Perley's Marsh. He took up his medical career again and also set up the Bracklesham Bay Riding School, as riding was one of his favourite pastimes. He used to ride along the beach for gallops as long as five miles as there were no groynes on the beach at that time.

However his war wounds still plagued

W. B. Allen's medals (R.A.M.C.)

him and he took to drink and drugs, as this was the only way that he could obtain relief. In 1932 he crashed his car in Bracklesham and was examined by a Police Surgeon at his home and found to be under the influence of drink. His solicitor told the court at Chichester of Allen's war record and said "he had been a physical wreck, nerves gone, and not being able to sleep, had taken to drugs and whisky". Allen had his licence suspended for five years and was fined a nominal £1.

On October 27th 1933 he was found in bed seriously ill by a member of the staff of his Riding Stables (Allen's wife was ill herself at the time and in a nursing home) who called for Doctor C. R. Sadler at 6.41 a.m. but at 7.15 when the doctor arrived it was too late to save Allen's life. At the subsequent inquest in Chichester,

Earnley Church, West Sussex (W. Fullaway)

the doctor testified that Allen had been taking luminol, opium, and morphia in unknown quantities, and when questioned the doctor considered that Allen was suffering from Opium poisoning. He died within 30 minutes of his arrival. The verdict on Allen's death was that of "misadventure" rather than suicide. Nearly fifteen years after the Great War finished it had claimed another victim.

Allen was given a 'hero's funeral' and was buried at Earnley Cemetery near Bracklesham. He is still remembered today according to the local press as "a slim clever man who was a very good doctor. He was a good and generous man and well liked locally."

Earnley Cemetery, West Sussex (W. Fullaway)

He married firstly Mary Young Mercer and later Gertrude who died in 1955. His medals are in the hands of the R.A.M.C.

T. Hughes

Guillemont September 3rd 1916

On September 3rd 1916, the British plan to capture Guillemont, the shambles that had once been a village, was for an advance in three stages. The British began their bombardment at 8.15 a.m. in order to pave the way for an attack and at

8.33 a.m. a special barrage was directed towards the north east of the village. On the extreme left of the 59th Bde. (20th Light Div.), the 10 K.R.R.C. pressed forward and was able to surprise the enemy. The 6th Connaught Rangers of the 47th Bde. (16th Irish) Div. wanted to get ahead and into the action as well. They followed the K.R.R.C. on the northern side of Mount Street. This 'street' was the former high street that ran through the centre of the village. At noon the rest of the line advanced. According to the *Official History* "The 10/K.R.R.C. was obliged to "mop up" in the area of the 6th Connaught Rangers (47th Brigade) on its left, for the impetuous Irishmen had swept on without quelling all resistance in the vicinity of the quarry." The quarry was to the left of Mount Street as the troops entered the village.

Pte. Thomas Hughes won a V.C. during this fighting as a member of the 6th Connaughts and his own account of the action was as follows:

"On the 3rd of September we went over the top. After being hit in four different places, I noticed a machine-gun

Hyde Park June 2nd 1917 (The Times)

firing in the German lines. So I rushed up, shot both the chaps on the gun and brought it back. I remember no more until I found myself down in the dressing station. P.S.I forgot to mention I brought four German prisoners with the gun."

His citation was published on October 26th 1916 and read as follows:

"For most conspicuous bravery and determination. He was wounded in an attack, but returned at once to the firing line after having his wounds dressed.

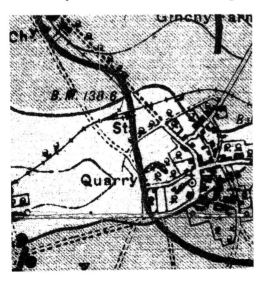

Hyde Park June 2nd 1917 (Ill. London News)

Later, seeing a hostile machine-gun, he dashed out in front of his company, shot the gunner, and single-handed captured the gun. Though again wounded, he brought back three or four prisoners."

In his book *War Letters to a Wife* Rowland Feilding of the Connaughts wrote on October 29th, 1916:

"We have our tails up to-day because we have just heard that Private Hughes, of this battalion, has been awarded the V.C. for his behaviour at Guillemont. It is *something* to have a V.C. belonging to your batallion!"

He was awarded his V.C. by the King at a special ceremony on June 2nd 1917 at Hyde Park. Hughes had to to use both his sticks to help him walk.

Broomfield, Co. Monaghan (M. Staunton)

Thomas Hughes was the son of Mr and

Mrs Hughes of County Monaghan and was born at Coravoo, near Castleblaney on May 30th 1885.

He was found dead at his home Fincairn, Broomfield, near Carrickmacross, Co. Monaghan, on January 8th 1942. He was 56 years of age, and was thought of as County Monaghan's own "Sergeant York". It is unlikely that he was able to work after the war because of his wounds, and he became increasingly dependent on drink. Indeed in 1924 he was fined for being in the possession of illegal liquor.

Hughes left his V.C. to his sister and in the late 1950s she found herself in reduced circumstances and took steps to sell her brother's medal. It was purchased by a London Dealer for £420 and as a result of a subscription by former members of the Connaught Rangers it was then bought for £500 and presented to the Sandhurst Military Museum, the Rangers having been disbanded in 1922. It was later passed on to the National Army Museum at Chelsea.

J. V. Holland

Lieut. JOHN V. HOLLAND, V.C.
Photo: Central News

Gallahers Cigarette Card

By the time that the German held village of Guillemont had been captured no less than five V.C. s had been awarded; to C.S.M. W. J. G. Evans, to Captain N. G. Chavasse and on the day of its actual capture, September 3rd 1916 to Lt. J. V. Holland, Pte. T. Hughes and Pte. D. Jones. Only the fight to capture the stronghold village of Thiepval was to rival the struggle that the Allies had with the capture of Guillemont. In both, five V.C. awards were won.

On September 3rd the 59th Bde. (20th Light Div.) and units of the 60th Bde. (20th. Light Div.) had the southern part of Guillemont as their objective. The 47th Bde. of the 16th (Irish) Div. were brought up to replace the 60th Bde. in the attack on the northern part of the village. On the left flank of the 16th Div. a "dashing assault" was delivered southeastward by the 7th Leinsters of the 47th Bde. The assault was led by Lt. J. V. Holland, the battalion bombing officer, who was attached from the 3rd Leinsters and it proved so successful that it virtually carried the day. The unit had attacked from the trenches beyond Guillemont Station and had carried "all before it".

Guillemont September 3rd 1916

Holland's citation was published on October 26th 1916 and tells the story as well as any other source:

"For most conspicuous bravery, during a heavy engagement, when not content with bombing hostile dug-outs within the objective, he fearlessly led his bombers through our own artillery barrage and cleared a part of the village in front.

He started out with 26 bombers and finished up with only five, after capturing some fifty prisoners. By this very gallant action he undoubtedly broke the spirit of the enemy, and saved us many casualties when the battalion made a further advance.

He was far from well at the time, and later had to go to hospital."

He was presented with his V.C. by the King at Buckingham Palace on February 5th 1917.

John Vincent Holland was the son of John Holland, M.R.C.V.S. and Katherine (formerly Peppard) of the Model Farm, Athy, County Kildare, Ireland. He was born on July 19th 1889, one of eight children. He went to school at Clongowes Wood College, at Naas, County Kildare and then to Liverpool University. He was a veterinary student but gave up his studies and his father paid for him to travel extensively in South America. He was involved with ranching, railway engineering and hunting. At the age of 25 he returned to England and enlisted as a trooper in the 2nd Life Guards on September 2nd 1914. He trained at Cumbermere Barracks, Windsor. Captain F. C. Hitchcock in his book *"Stand To"* says that Holland was nicknamed "Tin-Belly" as a result of his service with the Life Guards. He was granted a commission with the 3rd

Leinsters in February 1915 and was attached to the 2nd Royal Dublin Fusiliers and was wounded on the night of June 26th in the Second Battle of Ypres. He returned to England and Ireland in order to recover and when he went back to France he was attached to the 7th Leinsters, with whom he fought as Battalion Bombing Officer at Loos, Hulluch and the Somme in 1916. He had been made a full Lieutenant in July 1916. After Guillemont he was promoted to the rank of Captain. Later he was Mentioned in Despatches, and awarded "The Parchment Certificate of the Irish Division." After his award was announced General Hickie wrote a congratulatory letter to Holland's father and General Pereira wrote to Holland himself:

"My Dear Holland, ... I did not expect an answer to my telegram which I sent to show how much the Brigade appreciated the honour you had reflected on them by your gallant action at Guillemont, I am very glad that the bombers are also included-I think that two got the D.C.M. and six more the Military Medal. -so you will be able tc rejoice that the gallant men who went with you were not forgotten. We were all very sorry that you yourself were not present when the Battalion celebrated the event, and that you could not hear the cheers that were raised for you. I am sorry that you have been so seedy, but I hope that you are now picking up, and I hope that you will live long to wear the proudest distinction that can be awarded to a soldier."

One of Holland's Bombers Pte. A. Lee also wrote to him and quotes a few words that Holland had said on September 3rd 1916 at Guillemont: "Boys, a Victoria Cross is to be won".

Holland married Frances Grogan,

daughter of Joseph Grogan, J.P. of the Manor House, Queenstown, Rossleague. Grogan's business interests included the servicing of Royal Naval vessels at Queenstown where the Navy had a base during the War. The marriage took place at the Cathedral in Queenstown on January 15th 1917. The military wedding was a 'brilliant and impressive one . . . and the bridegroom's Regiment paid every military honour and courtesy to their first and only V.C. and his newly-wedded bride'. Holland was then made Staff Instructor, number 16, Officer Cadet Battalion, Kinnel Park, Rhyl.

After the war Holland joined the 9th Lancers in India where he was able to

Wedding January 15th 1917

carry on with his favourite pursuits of horseriding and hunting. He was appointed Major and was transferred to Kenya for a period of Colonial Service. By this time there were two sons in the

En route for London (The Sun May 24th 1956)

family and their English home was at 34, Elm Road, Seaforth, Merseyside. Holland returned from Kenya in 1936 and the family then moved and set up home in Colwyn Bay, Wales. Holland was employed in various Civil Service occupations, and in 1940 after the outbreak of the Second War, he returned to the Army in India but was invalided out in 1941. He then took up a position with the Ministry of Food. In the 1950s he and his wife emigrated to Tasmania where Frances died in 1960.

Holland who was a tall aristocratic looking man never really settled down to civilian life and was probably at his happiest when serving with the Army abroad. He visited London in 1956 with the Australian contingent for the Victoria Cross Review held in front of the Queen in Hyde Park. He died in Hobart, Tasmania at the age of 85 on February 27th 1975. He was buried at Cornelian Cemetery by the side of his wife on March 1st after a service of Requiem Mass at St. Mary's Cathedral. He was given a full military funeral.

His medals are in private hands.

D. Jones

The third man to be awarded the V.C. for gallantry on September 3rd, although it was posthumous, was Sgt. David Jones of the 12th King's (Liverpool Regiment). The 20th (Light) Division were ordered to take Guillemont on the 3rd and then establish a line 500 yards to the east of the village. The 61st Bde. which included the 12th King's were to be prominent in the fighting.

In the late afternoon of the 3rd it was known that the 7th Div. had entered

Gallahers Cigarette Card

Ginchy, to the north east of Guillemont. Measures were taken to protect the flank of the Corps by positioning troops astride the Guillemont-Ginchy Road, an initiative that according to the *Official History* 'owed much to a company commander of the 12th King's (61st Bde.). His battalion had been sent up to reinforce the 47th Bde. (16th Irish Div.).' Sgt. D. Jones at 5.30 p.m. and again at 6.30 p.m. helped to beat off two German counter attacks by rifle and Lewis gun fire. His platoon which belonged to C Company of the 12th which was well forward on the southern side of Ginchy was to beat off several more attacks before being

relieved on the 5th.

His citation was published on October 26th 1916 and read as follows:

"For most conspicuous bravery, devotion to duty, and ability displayed in the handling of his platoon.

The platoon to which he belonged was ordered to a forward position, and during the advance came under heavy machine gun fire, the officer being killed and the platoon suffering heavy losses.

Serjeant Jones led forward the remainder, occupied the position, and held it for two days and two nights without food or water, until relieved. On the second day he drove back three counter-attacks, inflicting heavy losses. His coolness was most praiseworthy. It was due entirely to his resource and example that his men retained confidence and held their post."

October 7th was the first day of the battle for the Transloy Ridges. The 20th (Light Div.) were in action and their 60th and 61st Bdes. had their jumping off points on the road that ran in a south easterly direction from Guedecourt towards Le Transloy. The fighting began at 1.45 p.m. and the 61st Bde., with the 7th K.O.Y.L.I. and the 12th King's to the fore made progress of about 500 yards, and into the western section of Rainbow Trench. David Jones was in number 10 platoon of the latter battalion and was killed in the fighting. At one point a number of Germans gave themselves up and those who retired towards Beaulencourt became easy targets. The two battalions even reached as far as a section of Cloudy Trench, a stretch of about 300 yards. However part of Rainbow Trench to their south east was still in enemy hands and so there was a danger in going forward too quickly. The 7th Somersets relieved the 12th King's later in the day. Jones' body was buried at Bancourt

Guillemont September 3rd 1916

British Cemetery, Plot V, Row F, grave 20.

His V.C. was presented to his widow Mrs D. Jones by the King at Buckingham Palace on March 31st 1917. The King asked Mrs Jones to wear the medal on the right breast, which she did although she was slightly embarrassed when soldiers saluted her!

David Jones was the son of David Jones and Jessie Jones, formerly Ginochio. He was born on January 10th 1891 at 3, Hutchinson Street, then in the West Derby district of Liverpool. His father was employed as a cotton porter, and later became a carrier with a grocery firm, Cooper & Co. Jones went to school at Heyworth Street School, Everton and later joined Blake's Motor Company,

Lord Street, Liverpool as a trainee motor mechanic.

He was 22 when war began in August 1914 and enlisted as a Private in the King's Liverpool Regiment at the end of August. On May 27th 1915 he married Elizabeth Dorothea Doyle and their home was 87, Heyworth Street. They had no family. In June he went to France. He was later promoted from being a Private and at the time of his death in October 1916 he was a Sergeant.

Nearly six months after he died two memorial tablets were unveiled, at Heyworth Street, School. One of the tablets a brass wall panel was erected inside the school and one made of granite was erected at the front of the school facing Heyworth Street. The ceremonies were attended by the Lord Mayor of

Bancourt British Cemetery (C.W.G.C.)

Liverpool and a large crowd. Those present included Jones' widow and other members of his family. The band of the 3rd Battalion Royal Welch Fusiliers led the singing of two hymns and played the *Last Post*. A contingent from the King's Regiment was also in attendance.

After the war was over Mrs Jones married a William J. Woosey, who was a plumber. When the King's Regiment merged with the Manchester Regiment she was not happy with the arrangement and presented David Jones' V.C. to his former employer, Blake's Motor Company. Each year a member of the firm travels to London and presents a wreath at the Cenotaph in Whitehall on Remembrance Sunday. In the 1970s the plaque in Heyworth School was moved to a position in Everton Park C. P. School.

Bancourt British Cemetery (D. C. Jennings)

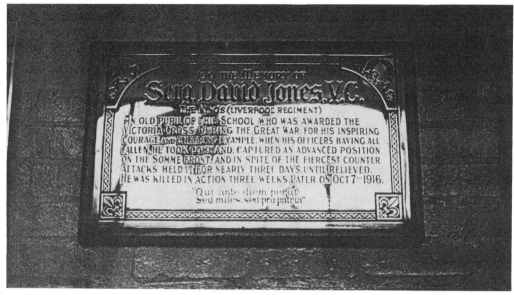

Plaque at Everton Park CP School

L. Clarke

In the six days between September 3rd and September 9th 1916, Pozieres Ridge had been finally taken by the Allies and there had been continuous fighting towards High Wood. Most of Leuze Wood towards Combles had been taken as had Falfemont Farm. Finally on September 9th itself the village of Ginchy was to fall into Allied hands after very hard fighting.

Back on the western side of the Somme battlefield the Australians and the Canadians were trying to move towards and capture Mouquet Farm as part of the plan to capture the German stronghold of Thiepval. The position to the north west of the Pozieres O. G. Trench lines was called Fabeck Graben which in early September had been lost by the Germans. Although Sir Douglas Haig wanted the Canadian Army to be allowed to 'settle in' before they were committed to the fray, there was little chance as the

Germans were not going to give up their positions in front of Mouquet Farm without a considerable fight.

In addition to relieving the Australians on the the Mouquet Farm Front the Canadian Army in the shape of the 2nd Canadian Battalion (lst Canadian Div.) were also ordered to attack on the south side of the Albert-Bapaume Road. Their objective was the German front trench astride the railway leading to Martin-puich. The fight continued on a front of 500 yards and more than 60 German prisoners were taken. However the line was continuously bombarded by the German artillery and there were several German counter attacks which were fought off. It was during this time that Cpl. L. Clarke of the 2nd Canadian Bn. won his V.C. He virtually attacked a party of 20 Germans on his own and routed them. He took one prisoner despite being seriously wounded in the leg by a German bayonet. The attack had begun at 4.45 p. m. and three companies of the battalion out of four made the assault. When they reached the enemy line they found that the Allied barrage had not been very successful, thus there were many Germans waiting for them.

Cpl. Clarke was ordered by Lt. Hoey to take part of a bombing section and clear out some of the enemy on the left flank. He was then to join up with Sgt. W. H. Nicholls at a block that the latter was to build. Clarke was the first to enter what turned out to be a strongly fortified

Gallahers Cigarette Card

position and he and the rest of his group bombed the Germans out of it. At this time a party of Germans including two officers advanced towards the Canadians along the trench. The Germans had already seen enough of Clarke's methods and had to be urged to the attack. Clarke took them all on with firstly the use of his revolver, and then he seized a German rifle and used that as well. The senior of the two German officers lunged at Clarke and wounded him severely just below the knee with his bayonet. It was the officer's last act as Clarke then shot him. The remaining five Germans turned and fled and even then Clarke pursued them hard. One who spoke excellent English surrendered and Clarke turned him over to Sgt. Nicholls who had managed to finish building the block. Lt. Hoey had to order Clarke to have his wounds attended to. Nevertheless Clarke returned next day to his platoon in billets.

Clarke continued in battle but his wounds became very serious and he was sent to Number One General Hospital, Etretat near Le Havre, where he died on October 19th. He was buried at Etretat

Near Pozieres September 9th 1916

Churchyard Plot 11, Row C, Grave 3A. The citation for his V.C. was published on October 26th a week later. It read as follows:

"For most conspicuous bravery. He was detailed with his section of bombers to clear the continuation of a newly-captured trench and cover the constuction of a "block". After most of his party had become casualties, he was building a "block" when about twenty of the enemy with two officers counter-attacked. He boldly advanced against them, emptied his revolver into them, and afterwards two enemy rifles, which he picked up in the trench.

One of the officers then attacked him with the bayonet, wounding him in the leg, but he shot him dead. The enemy then ran away, pursued by Acting Corporal Clarke, who shot four more and captured a fifth.

Later he was ordered to the dressing

station, but returned next day to duty."

Clarke's father Mr. H. T. Clarke received his son's posthumous V.C. at a ceremony in Winnipeg in 1917 from the hands of the Governor-General of Canada the 9th Duke of Devonshire.

Lionel Beaumaurice (Leo) Clarke was born on December 1st 1892 in Waterdown, Hamilton, Ontario. He was the son of Henry Trevelyan Clarke and Rosseta Caroline Nona Clarke, of 785 Pine Street, Winnipeg, Manitoba. His early years were spent in England but his parents returned to Winnipeg in the period 1903-1905. After leaving school Leo Clarke held a number of jobs and when war broke out in August 1914 he was working on the survey in the

Entretat Churchyard, France (D. C. Jennings)

Entretat Churchyard, France (C.W.G.C.)

Canadian north. He returned to Winnipeg and enlisted as a Private with the 27th Bn. C.E.F. on February 25th 1915. He left with them to sail to England and then to France in September. He transferred to the Second Canadian Bn., in order to be near his brother who was serving with the unit. Clarke was wounded for the first time at the end of 1915.

On August 6th 1916 he was made an Acting Corporal and with his unit moved south to the Somme battlefield at the beginning of September. The immediate goals were Mouquet Farm and the village of Courcelette, a mile behind the German front trenches.

On Sunday, September 19th 1971, at 2. p.m. a historical plaque to the memory of Cpl. Leo Clarke was unveiled in front of the Royal Canadian Legion Building, Hamilton Street, Waterdown, Ontario. Relatives of the Clarke family attended the ceremony. Clarke's medals are in private hands.

D. F. Brown

In between September 9th when Cpl. L. Clarke won his posthumously given V.C. and the 15th when three V.C.s were awarded, the Allies were making preparations for the third phase of the Battle of the Somme. It was to be a day of great progress and advances were made to the depth of two to three thousand yards on parts of the sixteen mile front. With the help of the first ever appearance of the Tank in battle the villages of Flers, Martinpuich, and Courcelette were taken. Even High Wood which was meant to have been captured in mid July fell to the British after two months of bitter struggle.

D. F. Brown

The New Zealand Division was given the task of capturing the series of trenches on the sloping ground between Delville and High Woods. The 2nd Aucklands and the 2nd Otagos of the 2nd New Zealand Bde went forward and the former battalion captured Coffee Trench easily but the Otagos met considerable enemy resistance at a position called Crest Trench. A German machine gun was in particular giving great trouble. Sgts D. F. Brown and J. Rodgers crawled forward to within 30 yards of the machine gun before rushing forward and killing the crew. The attackers then moved quickly on towards the Switch Trench virtually ignoring the Allied barrage which they were catching up with. Sgt. Brown and his company destroyed another German machine gun position and with the aid of bombs and bayonets the Switch Trench was captured. They next moved onto the Flers Line where they remained for five hours and Brown's company was almost totally decimated. The company eventually came out of the line, still with their two Sergeants, but only with 49 men.

Brown was awarded the V.C. for his heroism but was killed sixteen days later near Eaucourt l'Abbaye, on October 1st. As before Brown was in the thick of the fighting. The Otagos attacked Circus Trench which led to the Abbey Road in front of Eaucourt l'Abbaye. The artillery had pounded the German positions since early morning, and at one minute before zero hour, which was 3.15 p.m. about 60 oil mortars were fired which set fire to the German trenches and created a black oily smoke. The New Zealanders then charged the enemy on a front of 1800 yards. The 2nd Bde. penetrated to a depth of 800 yards. As on September 15th Brown took on a German machine gun crew and bayoneted them. However his luck finally ran out and he was shot by a machine gun and died of wounds. His citation was not gazetted until June 14th 1917 and read as follows:

"For most conspicuous bravery and determination in attack when the company to which he belonged suffered very heavy casualties in officers and men from machine gun fire.

At great personal risk this N.C.O.

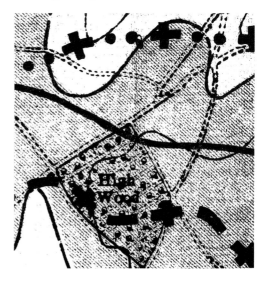

Warlencourt British Cemetery (C.W.G.C.)

advanced with a comrade and succeeded in reaching a point within thirty yards of the enemy guns. Four of the gun crew were killed and the gun captured.

The advance of the company was continued till it was again held up by machine gun fire. Again Sjt. Brown and his comrade with great gallantry rushed the gun and killed the crew. After this second position had been won, the company came under very heavy shell fire, and the utter contempt for danger and coolness under fire of this non-commissioned officer did much to keep up the spirit of his men. On a subsequent occasion in attack Sergeant Brown sho-wed most conspicuous gallantry. He attacked single-handed a machine gun which was holding up the attack, killed the gun crew and captured the gun. Later, while sniping the retreating enemy, this very gallant soldier was killed."

Brown was buried at Warlencourt

Warlencourt British Cemetery (D. C. Jennings)

British Cemetery near the Abbaye on the Bapaume Road, Plot 111, Row F, Grave 11. Robert Brown, Sgt. Brown's father was presented with his son's V.C. by His Excellency the Right Honourable The Earl of Liverpool, Governor-General of New Zealand at Oamaru on August 30th 1917.

———————

Donald Forester Brown was born in Dunedin, New Zealand on February 23rd 1890 and became a farmer. At the age of 25 he enlisted with the New Zealand Expeditionary Force on October 19th 1915. He embarked for Egypt with the 9th Reinforcements in January 1916. In April they left for France. His was the first V.C. to be won by a member of the New Zealand Forces in France. His other medals included the British War Medal and the Victory Medal. He is commemorated in New Zealand at the H.Q. Dunedin RSA. His medals are in private hands.

F. McNess

The Guards Division were based at Ginchy on September 15th from where they were to launch an attack towards Lesboeufs. At 6.20 a.m. when the creeping barrage began the Guards moved forward keeping 30 yards behind it. As they moved forward towards a position called The Triangle to the north east they were caught by terrific fire from the right where the Germans still held The Quadrilateral; at this point they were opposite the British 6th Division. All four battalions of the 2nd Guards Bde. reached The Triangle including the 1st Scots Guards. The numbers of all of the units were however very much depleted even though the battle had only lasted barely an hour. It was during this fighting that Lance-Sgt. Fred McNess earned his V.C. and was seriously wounded in the head and in other parts of his body.

    McNess described the event in a letter home that was printed in the local papers in Leeds a few weeks later:

    "after getting through a small opening in the barbed wire in front of the German Trench, I took a party up the communication trench, and for an hour and a half a corporal and I slowly but surely drove the enemy back. The remainder of the boys

Gallahers Cigarette Card

passed the bombs to us, we being the only two who could use them. Then we ran short, but finding large quantities of

German bombs we experimented with them until we found out how to use them. Then we fought them with their own bombs. It was a case of hand-to-hand fighting all the way up. Then I got wounded. It was like this. One of the men in my platoon was shot through the lungs. . . I was just preparing another bomb when a German threw a bomb which burst right in front of my dial. . . (McNess had the left side of his neck and part of his jaw, his lower teeth and some of his upper teeth blown away by the German bomb) I had to walk two miles to the first field dressing station. Here I received a rough dressing, then German prisoners carried me three miles to the ambulance. (At one stage he was treated by Noel Chavasse). I underwent an operation at the first hospital I came to then another one at Rouen (9th General Hospital), one on the day I arrived here, and I have another coming off tomorrow, it is just a case of straightening up old repairs."

The "official version" of McNess's heroism was published in a citation dated October 26th 1916 and read as follows:

"For most conspicuous bravery. During a severe engagement he led his men on with the greatest dash in the face of heavy shell and machine gun fire. When the first line of enemy trenches was reached, it was found that the left flank was exposed and that the enemy was bombing down the trench.

Sergeant McNess thereupon organised a counter attack and led it in person. He was very severely wounded in the neck and jaw but went on passing through the barrage of hostile bombs in order to bring up fresh supplies to his own men.

Finally he established a "block, and continued encouraging his men and throwing bombs till utterly exhausted by loss of blood".

McNess was later under surgery at King George's Hospital, Stamford Street, London where the surgeons used part of his rib to reconstruct his jaw. At this time he was summoned to receive

Near Ginchy September 15th 1916

his V.C. and was driven from the hospital to Buckingham Palace on December 9th 1916. He was accompanied by a Sergeant of the R.A.M.C. At the Palace he was greeted by Colonel Fludyer till recently commander of the Scots Guards who conducted McNess to the Royal presence. An observer said that McNess' appeared to be in a very sorry plight, though exceedingly cheerful. He was badly wounded in the neck, arm, shoulder and side. 'McNess was with the King for about twenty minutes while the story of what had happened was read out. The King talked to him and expressed concern about his wounds. McNess was decorated after the Generals and was the only V.C. holder to be presented on that day.'

F. McNess

Fred McNess was born in Bramley, Leeds on January 22nd 1892. He was the son of John McNess of Perth who served at one time with the Royal Engineers and of Mary McNess. There were three sons and one daughter in the family. Fred went to Bramley National School and grew up to be a well set up and strapping young man, he was five foot nine in height. He was also a great walker and nature lover and used to ramble through the Wharfedale valleys at weekends. He was a carter's assistant before the war and enlisted with the 3rd (Reserve) Battalion of the Scots Guards in London on January 10th 1915. He was appointed unpaid Corporal on February 7th 1916 and left for France to join the 1st Bn. on April 6th 1916. He was made up to Corporal (Lance Sergeant) on August 25th 1916.

After he was presented with the V.C. in December 1916 he was sent for a time to convalesce at Welbeck Abbey but soon returned to King George's Hospital where he was to remain for eighteen

months. In mid July 1917 McNess received an official welcome at Leeds and in his home town of Bramley near Leeds and crowds of people turned out to greet him. In the evening a brass band led a parade through the streets of the town. In October 1917 McNess was presented with a massive clock and sidepieces in bronze by Colonel J. W. Smith-Neill, Commander of the Scots Guards at Wellington Barracks. On June 14th 1918 he finally left King George's when he was discharged from the Army with a pension as not being physicaly fit enough for Army duties. In early January 1920 he was again feted by his home town as were other members of the returned forces. However McNess was presented with an Illuminated Address and the sum of £400 which allowed him to start up a shoe repair business at 95 Woodhouse Lane, Leeds. Arrangements had also been made for him to be trained for this profession. His widowed mother lived at the family home at 35 Eightlands Lane, Bramley, Leeds.

Until he retired McNess lived at 6 Springbank Crescent, Headingley, Leeds and latterly worked on the staff of the Leeds City Engineers Department as a filing clerk. In 1939 he wrote to the Scots Guards about the possibility of a recall and was thanked but politely turned down because the injuries he had received in the Great War made him medically unfit for service. On his retirement at the age of 64 he and his wife decided to move to the South Coast and bought a bungalow at 37 Petersfield Road, Boscombe, Hants in January 1956.

On May 5th while his wife Dorothy was out of the house he took his own life. Although no one can know his actual state of mind at the time I think that it can be assumed that he was in a period of deep depression, a depression which must have had its roots in his very severe war wounds suffered nearly 40 years before. Possibly his move to the south of England had an unsettling effect on him as well. At the inquest Mrs McNess gave evidence that "her husband was badly wounded in the First War and had suffered depression and headaches." The Coroner's verdict was "that he took his life while the balance of his mind was disturbed". McNess' funeral took place at Bournemouth on May 8th and his medals were displayed on the coffin. Later McNess was cremated.

Unfortunately his suicide was not only a tragedy in itself but the Ministry of Pensions and National Insurance chose to ignore the root cause of it and immediately suspended Mrs McNess' right to her late husband's pension. Their reason for doing this was the manner of McNess'

death, and the lack of real proof that McNess's wounds were the sole cause of his death. Mrs McNess was faced with living on her widow's pension of just £2 per week. However there is a redeeming element in all this and that is the role that McNess' Regiment played. Dorothy McNess wrote to them for assistance at the outset of her problems from an address at 11 Cecil Court, Charminston Road, Bournemouth. As a result she was paid £10 per month out of Regimental Funds.

Mrs McNess was invited to appeal which she did. The Scots Guards also took a hand and wrote directly to John Boyd-Carpenter, an ex Guardsman who was the Minister responsible.

McNess' former doctor from Leeds wasn't much help either as "he felt that he could not relate the war injury directly to his suicide partly as McNess never spoke of the war." Before he died McNess had prostate trouble and an ulcer on his face and died shortly after moving into his new house. Several witnesses of McNess' shyness and unwillingness to talk about the war mention this fact in reports of his death. The negotiations that Mrs McNess had with the Ministry went on for about a year and at the same time she was also trying to sell her new home. Unfortunately nobody wished to buy the property owing to its unfortunate associations. At one point contracts had actually been exchanged but at the last minute the wife of the man buying the property suddenly died and the sale fell through.

However this story does have a happy ending and Boyd-Carpenter was able to write to the Scots Guards telling them that the appeal had been successful (June 18th 1957). The pension was backdated to McNess' death a year before and in time the bungalow was sold and Mrs

McNess went to live with her family. She was naturally overjoyed about the outcome of her appeal and she received her new pension book on July 15th 1957 and wrote off immediately to the Regiment.

In 1956 Mrs McNess had also mentioned to the Regiment that her late husband had always expressed the wish that they should have his medals after his death and they were duly presented. Apart from the V.C. he had been awarded the British War Medal, Victory Medal, Kings Certificate No 843, War Badge and Certificate 925. The Regiment were very grateful to receive the medals and promised to look after them. At the end of 1956 McNess' V.C. was part of an exhibition of Yorkshire V.C.s held in Leeds. This would have been part of the centenary of the founding of the Victoria Cross Medal.

At the H.Q. of the 1st Scots Guards in Germany (1990) a painting of McNess' action in September 1916 is on display, a copy of it is to be seen at Wellington Barracks, Birdcage Walk, London.

J. V. Campbell

Maj. & Bre. Lt.-Col. J. V. CAMPBELL, V.C
Photo: Farringdon

Gallahers Cigarette Card

Three V.C.s were to be awarded on September 15th; to Donald Brown of the New Zealand Division in the struggle for the trenches between Delville and High Woods, to Fred McNess (lst Scots Guards 2nd Gds. Bde.) for bombing the Germans out of their positions north east of Ginchy and to Lt. Col. J. V. Campbell of the 3rd Coldstream Guards (lst Gds. Bde.) for taking personal command of a third line of his battalion when the first two waves had been decimated.

The Guards Division were occupying the village of Ginchy on September 15th and the overall Fourth Army Plan in this part of the Somme battlefield was to capture the enemy defences between Morval and Le Sars. The southern limit of the Guards Division attack was 500 yards south of the Ginchy-Les Boeufs road. The plan was that the 2nd and 3rd Coldstream (1st Gds. Bde.) were to advance and occupy the first three objectives, then the 1st Irish Gds. of the same brigade were to pass through the captured lines and reach the fourth line which was named the Red Line. Opposition was expected from the left flank and the 2nd Grenadier Gds. were ordered to form a defensive flank on this left side of the attack.

The infantry of the 1st Bde went forward at zero hour which was 6.20 a.m. and was in trouble from the start and the first waves of the Coldstreams were literally mown down. The enemy were positioned with machine guns in the Flers-Ginchy sunken road and inflicted great damage on one of the British Army's crack units. Major Vaughan second in command of the 3rd Coldstreams was killed as was their Adjutant. They had not even covered 100 yards of ground. The infantry tried to deal with the attackers in the sunken road although tanks had been assigned to this task but had failed to show up.

Lt. Col. Campbell in charge of the 3rd Coldstreams realized that there would be no progress until the sunken road was cleared and the attack on the left flank pressed home. He had with him his hunting horn from his time with the Shropshire Harriers and blew just one note on it, which was sufficient to rally the wavering troops who then moved forward in an irresistible rush. The Guardsmen carried the sunken road and went down the slope of one valley and up the slope of another. Finally they reached as far as the German Third Line. The position had been captured at 7.15 a.m. The infantry were not to attack further until their right flank had been protected. However it was discovered that they were not after all in the German Third Line but in fact in the enemy First Line, this meant that it was important to press on and the Coldstreams were ordered to move forward in the direction of the church at Les Boeufs, which was then visible The

Ginchy September 15th 1916

troops advanced but were almost immediately checked by intense enemy fire and for a second time that morning Campbell sounded his hunting horn.

This time the German Third Line was really reached and Campbell wanted to press on and capture Les Boeufs and sent a message back for reinforcements to be sent up. However General Feilding in charge of the attack would not allow this, as the 6th Div. on the left flank had not made progress and any forward thrust by the Guards would leave them dangerously exposed to a serious counter attack. Instead the positions known as the Blue Line were to be consolidated.

Not surprisingly Campbell was awarded the V.C. for taking command of the situation and in saving the day for the Guards. Despite their success in terms of

J. V. Campbell

Punch (November 22nd 1916)

ground covered it was at a huge cost of human life. The award was published on October 26th 1916 and read as follows:

"For most conspicuous bravery and able leading in an attack.

Seeing that the first two waves of his battalion had been decimated by machine gun and rifle fire he took personal command of the third line, rallied his men with the utmost gallantry, and led them against the enemy machine guns, capturing the guns and killing the personnel.

Later in the day, after consultation with other unit commanders, he again rallied the survivors of his battalion, and

J. V. Campbell in 1922

at a critical moment led them through a very heavy hostile fire barrage against the objective.

He was one of the first to enter the enemy trench.

His personal gallantry and initiative at a very critical moment turned the fortunes of the day and enabled the division to press on and capture objectives of the highest tactical importance."

On November 14th Campbell was presented with his V.C. by the King at Buckingham Palace and on the 16th he was transferred from being the C.O. of the 3rd Coldstream Gds. of the 137th Bde. (46th North Midland Territorial Div.), a position he held until November 7th 1918.

John Vaughan Campbell was born into a military family on October 31st 1876 in

Benwell House, Woodchester, nr Stroud (W. Oliver Wicks)

London. His father was the Hon. Ronald
Campbell and his mother was formerly
Katherine Claughton, daughter of
Bishop Claughton of St. Albans. John
was also the grandson of the 2nd Earl of
Cawdor.

Ronald Campbell was killed in the
Zulu War and John was sent to Eton and
then Sandhurst. He joined the Coldstream Guards on September 5th 1896
when he was nearly 21 years of age. He
was made a Lieutenant on April 6th 1898
and Adjutant to the Regiment on December 29th 1900. He served in the South
African War and took part in the advance
on Kimberley in addition to other
engagements. He was awarded the
D.S.O. in 1901 and was promoted to
Captain on June 27th 1903 and Major on
June 21st 1913. On July 29th just before
the Great War began he was made
Temporary Lieut. Col. and given the
Brevet of that rank on January 1st 1916,
and full Lt. Colonel on November 29th
1917.

Before the war he lived at Broom Hall,
Oswestry, Shropshire and was Master of
the Tanat Side Harriers. He was a well
known rider to hounds and had ridden in
many steeplechases. He married Amy
Dorothy Penn daughter of John Penn,
M.P. on July 18th 1904 at the Chapel at
Wellington Barracks, Birdcage Walk.
They had two children, Diana and John

J. V. Campbell ("Tally Ho VC")

*Benwell House, Woodchester, nr Stroud (W.
Oliver Wicks)*

Ronald who became a Major with the
Coldstreams and was killed in May 1940.
John Campbell was made G.O.C. 3rd
Guards Bde. on November 8th 1918 and
during the war had been mentioned three
times in Despatches and awarded the
Legion of Honour as well as the Croix de
Guerre and C.M.G. In 1919 he was
appointed A.D.C. to the King and

retired from this post in 1933 and was then given the Honorary rank of Brigadier General. He unveiled the war memorial at Bellenglise which was on the site of a former German machine gun emplacement and was one of seven holders of the V.C. at the unveiling of the Guards Memorial opposite Horse Guards Parade, London. When he rode to hounds in the 1920s he still took with him his famous hunting horn.

His wife had died in 1927 and at her funeral her body was conveyed by farm wagon from Broom Hall, Oswestry to Trefonen for burial. He remarried Margaret Emily Robina, a daughter of Dr. and Mrs. A. Tennyson-Smith and moved to the Stroud District of Gloucestershire in 1937. In August 1939 just before the Second War began Campbell served as a Honorary Flight Lieutenant in the R.A.F. Volunteer Reserve until February 1941. He then took over command of the 8th Gloucestershire Btn. Home Guard, a position that he held for four years until his death in 1944. On Saturday May 20th he took the salute at Dursley in connection with "Salute the Soldier" week and two days later in the morning of May 22nd he died suddenly at his home at Benwell House, Woodchester, Stroud. His body was cremated at Cheltenham Crematorium and his ashes taken to Scotland where they were scattered into the River Findhorn off the Banchor Bridge, Drynechan on the Cawdor Estate. A memorial plaque was later erected on one of the walls of Cawdor Parish Church to his memory.

His second wife outlived him by 41, years dying on November 11th 1985. His V.C. and his hunting horn had been bequeathed to the Coldstreams and his other medals are on loan to them. Throughout his life after 1916 Campbell was always known as the "Tallyho V.C."

J. C. Kerr

Zollern Graben on the crest of a ridge formed one of the major enemy strongholds in the German Second Position. It was a north westerly position between Mouquet Farm to the south west and the village of Courcelette to the north east which had nearly been totally captured on September 15th 1916 by the Canadian Army. In particular the much fought for Sugar Refinery had at last fallen to the attackers. They had also overrun Mouquet Farm itself but did not totally clear it and were subsequently driven out.

The enemy from the Zollern positions had a clear view of any attackers and could enfilade adjoining trenches with machine gun fire. The 3rd Canadian Division was given these positions to capture on the evening of the 16th. The Division was made up of the 7th, 8th and 9th Canadian Bdes. The 7th were to strike at Fabeck Graben which was part of a trench which ran from Courcelette to Mouquet Farm. If successful the 9th Bde. were then to carry on to attack the Zollern from the east. The first part of the plan failed because the artillery overshot but two bombing parties of the 7th Bde. were able to enter the Fabeck Trench from both ends, thus sealing off a party of Germans, in a section of the trench which measured 250 yards. The defenders were in an impossible position as if they retreated they would be cut down by the Canadians to the left and right flanks. It was at this point that Pte. John Kerr of the 49th Btn. (7th Bde.) was to win the V.C. He moved forward as bayonet man

Gallahers Cigarette Card

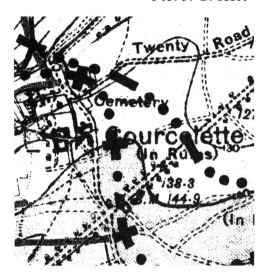

large party of attackers. That night Mouquet Farm was attacked again and the 2nd British Corps began to relieve the Canadian Division.

Kerr's citation was published on October 26th 1916 and read as follows:

"For most conspicuous bravery. During a bombing attack he was acting as a

in advance of his companions, he climbed over a block and moved thirty yards along the enemy position before being challenged. Eventually he was seen and a grenade was thrown at him, and in defending himself with his arm he lost part of his right fore-finger and was injured in his right side. There then ensued a bombing fight between the Canadians and the Germans but Kerr obviously grew impatient and wanted to hurry up the capture of the German position. He then ran along the top of the Fabeck Trench and fired down at its defenders killing several. The remaining 62 Germans surrendered. Although Kerr acted mostly on his own, the Germans probably thought that he was part of a

Courcelette September 16th 1916

bayonet man, and, knowing that bombs were running short, he ran along the parados under heavy fire until he was in close contact with the enemy, when he opened fire on them at point blank range, and inflicted heavy loss.

The enemy, thinking they were surrounded, surrendered. Sixty-two prisoners were taken and 250 yards of enemy trench captured.

Before carrying out this very plucky act one of Private Kerr's fingers had been blown off by a bomb.

Later, with two other men, he escorted back the prisoners under fire, and then returned to report himself for duty before having his wound dressed."

He received his V.C. from the King on February 5th 1917.

John Chipman Kerr was born at Fox River Cumberland County, Nova Scotia on January 11th 1887. Before the war he had moved north west of his birth place in order to become a farmer. He purchased some virgin land at Spirit River. After the war began however Kerr and a small group of other "homesteaders" walked 50 miles to the nearest railway and arrived at Edmonton where they enlisted in the 66th Bn.

At the beginning of June 1916 when being trained in England 400 men of the 66th were transferred to the 49th (Edmonton) Bn. who were in Belgium in

J. C. Kerr (National Archives of Canada)

the area of Sanctuary Wood near Ypres. The Canadians later went south to the Somme battlefield arriving at Albert on September 13th 1916. Less than 48 hours later they took up positions at a point near the Sunken Road in front of and to the west of the village of Courcelette.

After the war Kerr returned to Canada and died at Port Moody, British Columbia on February 19th 1963 at the age of 76. His V.C. is in the possession of the Alberta Provincial Museum.

T. A. Jones

After the Allied successes of mid September not a great deal happened in the way of ground captured but all this changed on the 25th when the battle was continued in earnest. Lesboeufs and Morval were both captured and subsequently Combles to the south east became

hemmed in by the British and the French.

On the right flank the 56th (London) Division were facing the west side of Combles and Bouleaux Wood. To their left was the 5th Division, and then came the 6th Division and the Guards Division. The 5th, 6th and Guards Divisions were

Gallahers Cigarette Card

Morval and then the lst Norfolks (15th Bde.) took the German support line half way up the slope to Morval. The Cheshires took the eastern side of Morval itself and the 16th R. Warwicks took the final objective a position from which observation could be had over Le Trans-loy and Sailly-Saillisel. The Cheshires arrived at their objective at about 2.55 p.m. and began immediately to consol-date their positions. It was at this point of the fighting that Private T. A. Jones was to gain his V.C.

Some German snipers were still active and Jones was stung by the loss of a friend to the German marksmen and set off to 'settle the score'. Jones succeeded with interest and managed to capture 102 prisoners including four officers. He had been shot twice by a sniper, once in his coat and once through his helmet, despite this he was uninjured, and managed to kill his assailant. He had been warned about the enemy misusing the white flag and took on two Germans who were using the flag but firing at him. He shot them both and continued on until he came to some enemy dugouts and partly

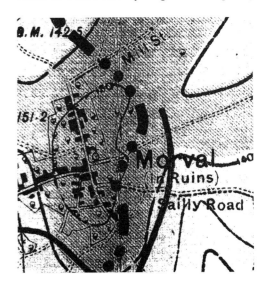

ordered to attack the line Morval-Lesboeufs, which if successful would allow Combles to be taken. For the moment we are concerned here with the progress of the lst Cheshires of the 15th Bde. of the 5th Division. They were situated between the 95th Bde., with their right on the Ginchy-Morval road and the 16th Bde of the 6th Division. The Cheshires had had only ten days to recover from some strenuous fighting near Falfemont Farm to the south west of Combles. The lst Bedfords (15th Bde.) took the German front line position at the bottom of the slope between Ginchy and dug trenches. He shot two officers and managed to disarm the rest of the occupants and then rounded them up. He brought them in with the help of four of his comrades. All this was within about 150 yards of the Cheshires' position and was seen by at least eleven officers who were to recommend the award of the Victoria Cross. The day had gone well for the Allies and the British had advanced over 2000 yards and as a result Combles fell without the necessity of a direct attack.

Morval September 25th 1916

Thomas Jones' citation was published on October 26th 1916 and read as follows:

"For most conspicuous bravery. He was with his company consolidating the defences in front of a village, and, noticing an enemy sniper at 200 yards distance, he went out, and, though one bullet went through his helmet, and another through his coat, he returned the sniper's fire and killed him. He then saw two more of the enemy firing at him, although displaying a white flag. Both of these he also shot. On reaching the enemy trench he found several occupied dug-outs, and, single-handed, disarmed 102 of the enemy, including three or four officers, and marched them back to our lines through a heavy barrage. He had been warned of the misuse of the white flag by the enemy, but insisted on going out after them."

Jones was presented with his V.C. by the King at Buckingham Palace on November 18th 1916.

Thomas Alfred Jones was born on Christmas Day 1880 at 39, Princess St. Runcorn, Cheshire. His father was Edward Jones. Thomas went to the local National School, and later joined the Runcorn Volunteers (Earl of Chester's Rifles) which he was with for 14 years. By trade he was a fitter and began work at Hazlehursts as a fitter and turner. After the completion of his apprenticeship he

V.C. WHO CAPTURED 102 GERMAN PRISONERS.

T. A. Jones November 1916

The Wide World April 1917

and a pair of field glasses. He was also given a civic reception at Chester and a dinner by his regiment. His parents did not miss out either as they were awarded an annual annuity by Jones' employer. His deed of capturing 102 German prisoners captured the public imagination and was written up in many national as well as provincial newspapers. It was mentioned in *The Times History of the War* and in a strange journal called *The Wide World* which was described as The Magazine For Men. In April 1917 an account based on an interview with Jones himself was published under the title of "Todger Jones, V.C." The Man who, Captured a Hundred Germans single handed. His own wonderful story as told by himself. The magazine also said that it could be sent free to soldiers and sailors from any Post Office.

At this time he was described as a quiet unasuming sort of man, he was smallish in

went to work with the Salt Union Company at their works at Weston Point, Runcorn. When war broke out in 1914 Jones was the second man to enlist with the lst Cheshires in Runcorn Drill Hall on August 5th and was sent to Birkenhead for training. The battalion left for the Western Front on August 16th and Jones found himself in the region of Hill 60 in Belgium for a period of four and a half months. During this time he was wounded twice but wasn't invalided home.

A few months after being awarded the V.C. he was officially welcomed home to Runcorn. He was given a tremendous ovation and was showered with gifts, presentations and honours. Amongst the gifts that he received were; a gold wrist watch, a silver teapot, a case of cutlery,

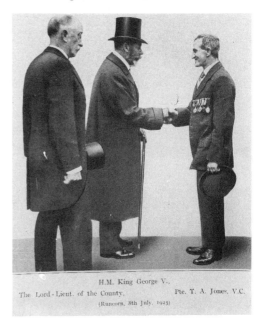

H.M. King George V.,
The Lord - Lieut. of the County,   Pte. T. A. Jones, V.C.
(Runcorn, 8th July, 1925)

T. A. Jones with King George Vth, Runcorn July 8th 1925 (The Times)

T. A. Jones' Funeral February 3rd 1956 (Runcorn Weekly News)

stature and very lithe. He had always been interested in football and at school was known on and off the field as Dodger Jones. Later as his christian name was Thomas this became "Todger" a name which stuck with him for the rest of his life. After Jones won the V.C. his gallantry was not exhausted for on September 28th 1918 he was to add the D.C.M. to his tally. This time the citation was as follows:

"For his utter fearlessness of danger and carrying messages safely through intense barrage fire, also guiding his comrades to their proper positions."

On demobilization he returned to work at the Salt Works at Runcorn, where he was to remain for 36 years all told before retiring. In 1928 a film company based on Wardour Street, London had the idea of producing a film called "For Valour". It was to be a film about how the War V.Cs had been won. The firm wrote to many of the surviving V.C. holders and there are letters on file between Jones and the film company. However there was such a public outcry against the project that it was decided to drop it.

His firm was taken over by I.C.I. and he retired in 1949. In 1954 he was present at a ceremony to mark the return of the lst Cheshire Battalion from a tour of duty in the Middle East. He was one of the guests at the saluting base as the troops marched past. He had always lived at 39 Princess Street and his elder sister Mrs E. Lightfoot had looked after him there since their parents had died. On January 4th 1956 he was admitted to the Victoria Memorial Hospital, Runcorn with cardiac problems. He died there a few weeks later at the age of 75 on January 30th. For his funeral that took place on February 3rd, the whole of Runcorn turned out to pay homage to their V.C. hero "Todger" Jones. The pavements were lined with people between his house at Princess Street and the church where the funeral service took place, St. Michaels. Flags flew at half mast and the coffin was draped with the Union Jack, Jones' war medals were displayed on the coffin. He was buried across the road from the church at Runcorn Cemetery, and was given a full military funeral.

After his death his sister Mrs Lightfoot presented her brother's medals to the Cheshire Regimental Museum at Chester Castle where they are on permanent display. In addition to the V.C. Jones had won, as we have seen, the D. C. M. and had also been given the 1914 Star, the British War Medal and the Victory Medal. As an expression of their gratitude the regiment wrote an official letter

Runcorn Cemetery

of thanks to Mrs Lightfoot and gave her a small brooch incorporating the Regimental badge. They also paid for and arranged for a small memorial in white marble about ten inches high in the shape of the V.C. to be placed on the family grave where Jones was buried. A short service was held when this memorial was dedicated on June 17th and the Chaplain to the local British Legion was in attendance; unfortunately Mrs Lightfoot was too ill to attend the short service but a younger sister of "Todger" was there. Jones is also commemorated in a memorial on the floor of Chester Cathedral. His grave fell into a bad state of repair and has recently been restored.

F. J. Edwards and R. E. Ryder

September 26th 1916 brought more good news for the Allies. On the day before, Morval and Lesboeufs had both been captured and on the 26th Combles was taken as was most of the German fortress village of Thiepval. Thiepval had been an objective for the July 1st attack nearly

thirteen weeks before it finally fell on the 27th.

The Middlesex Regiment was to win two V.C.s with its 12th battalion, one by Pte. F. J. Edwards and the second by Pte. R. E. Ryder. Not surprisingly the two men were to become great friends for the rest of their lives.

The 18th (Eastern) Div. were positioned to the north east of Authuille and faced the south west face of the village of Thiepval. On their left the 49th Div. was based on Thiepval Wood facing the west side of Thiepval. We are concerned here with the 54th Bde. whose battalions were made up of the 11th Royal Fusiliers, the 7th Bedfords, the 6th Northamptons and finally the 12th Middlesex. According to the *Official History*: "To the 54th Bde. fell one of the most difficult tasks of the day: the capture of the western half of Thiepval and the original German front system. The final objective was Schwa-

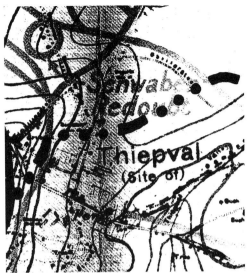

ben Redoubt, which crowned the top of the ridge nearly half a mile beyond the village."

The Middlesex Bn. was to attack on what was a narrow frontage and was to go through Thiepval. A company of the 11th R. Fus. was to advance up to the German front system and to also mop up behind the Middlesex. The 6th Northamptons were to help with clearing the Schwaben Redoubt and the 7th Bedfords were to be held in reserve. Two tanks concealed in Caterpillar Copse, to the south of Thiepval Wood were also to move forward as far as Thiepval Chateau, to the south west of the village. The assault began well and the Middlesex got as far as the Chateau where they were checked until one of the tanks crushed the German resistance. The right side of the Middlesex Bn. then moved forward while the left side was held up. In the early afternoon the German artillery caught the supporting Northamptonshire Bn.

At 2.30. p.m. Lt. Col. F. A. Maxwell commander of the Middlesex Bn. established his H.Q. at Thiepval Chateau, and

Gallahers Cigarette Card

Thiepval September 26th 1916

critical point Pte. R. Ryder, also of B Company, cleared a German trench when he brought a Lewis gun into action under a hail of bullets. Both men were awarded the V.C. and Ryder's award included his gallant conduct in later fighting. The three front line battalions had a total of 840 casualties out of 2,290 men. Edwards was recommended for the V.C. by Brigadier-General Maxwell. The citation was published on November 25th 1916 and read as follows:

"For most conspicuous bravery and resource. His part of the line was held up by machine-gun fire, and all officers had become casualties. There was confusion and indication of retirement.

Private Edwards, grasping the situation, on his own initiative dashed out alone towards the gun, which he knocked out with bombs.

reported this situation to Brigade. A defensive barrage was put down on an east-west line through the cemetery in mid afternoon and the 6th Northamptons began to arrive in support of the beleaguered battalions. Maxwell had assumed command of men from all three battalions and when darkness fell the German front trenches as well as the north west corner of the village were still in German hands. The attack was called off for the time being and summing up, the day's operations had resulted in a partial success. The 54th Bde. had done all that it could and the enemy had 'fought to the death.' Private Edwards of B. Company of the 12th Middlesex Bn. had at one point in the fighting rushed forward alone and bombed out a German machine gun position which had been holding up the advance. At a similarly

F. J. Edwards (Middlesex Regt.)

This very gallant act, coupled with great presence of mind and a total disregard of personal danger, made further advance possible and cleared up a dangerous situation."

Edwards was presented with his V.C. by the King on February 5th 1917.

Private Ryder's citation was also published on November 25th and read as follows:

"For most conspicuous bravery and initiative during an attack.

His company was held up by heavy rifle fire, and also his officers had become casualties. For want of leadership the attack was flagging.

Private Ryder realizing the situation, without a moment's thought for his own safety dashed absolutely alone at the enemy trench, and, by skilful manipulation of his Lewis gun, succeeded in clearing the trench. This very gallant act not only made possible, but also greatly inspired the subsequent advance and turned possible failure into success."

Ryder was awarded his V.C. at Buckingham Palace on November 29th four days after it was announced.

Frederick Jeremiah Edwards was born in Queenstown, County Cork on October 3rd 1894. He was the son of Quarter-Master Sergeant Henry J. Edwards of the Royal Garrison Artillery and of Mrs Anne Edwards. He was educated at the Royal Hibernian Military School, Phoenix Park Dublin which was a school for the sons of soldiers, he was also taught drumming. He joined the R.G.A. on October 30th 1908 when he was 14 years old. He was with the artillery in Hong Kong before transferring to the Middlesex Regiment. With the Middlesex he joined the newly formed 12th Battalion as a drummer, and became the second drum-

F. J. Edwards with his daughter

mer in the Regiment to be awarded the V.C. At some point he returned to his old school at Dublin where a presentation was made which included a solid silver flask and a cheque for the investment of War Loan certificates. In February 1918 the 12th Middlesex were disbanded and Edwards transferred to the Royal Fusiliers, he was promoted to the rank of Sergeant. In April 1918 he was taken prisoner by the Germans close to Amiens on the Somme. He was demobilized on March 20th 1921, and had several jobs before becoming mace bearer to the

F. J. Edwards with his mother circa 1917

Mayor of Holborn in London. In 1928 he was hard up and pawned his V.C. ; when a national newspaper came to hear of this they organised its recovery, only for Edwards to sell it again when he was short of money. In 1954 he suffered a stroke which seriously effected his mobility and he could only walk with the aid of a tripod stick, and then only for short distances. His speech too was affected. In April 1955 he became a resident of the Royal Star and Garter Home at Richmond, Surrey. The home had been formerly a hotel and the deeds for it were presented to Queen Mary in 1916. It opened its doors to 65 wounded men who mainly occupied the former banqueting hall and ballroom. After the war it was converted into a hospital with proper facilities and

Mace Bearer to the Mayor of Holborn

now houses 200 men from the three services. Running it cost just over £11,000 in 1916 and today the annual upkeep is over £2,000,000. Edwards used a wheel chair when away from the home.

In May 1963 he was present at Horse Guards Parade when the Middlesex Regiment held a ceremony there. On March 7th 1964 he had an severe attack of bronchitis, and appeared to be recovering when he had an acute coronary thrombosis and died 35 minutes past noon on March 9th. He was 69.

A detachment of the Middlesex Regiment provided an escort for Edwards' coffin when he was given a full military funeral and at the Soldier's Plot Richmond Cemetery where he was buried on March 16th. Amongst the mourners were several veterans including T.W.H. Veale V.C. and Bob Ryder V.C. Edwards' lifelong friend and pal who also had difficulty with walking and hobbled along behind the coffin with the use of sticks. Ryder,

Royal Star and Garter Home

Royal Star and Garter Home

F. J. Edwards with his great friend R. E. Ryder at Horse Guards, Whitehall 1963

F. J. Edwards wearing "fake" V.C.

were being offered for sale by auction. The Regiment wrote to their present and past members and asked what they thought that they could contribute to a purchase fund and also what they thought

also aged 69 had journeyed from Hucknall to attend the funeral and wore his medals in honour of his dead friend. The *Last Post* and *Reveille* were played by two regimental buglers.

Edwards had sold his medals eventually at a time when he was hard up, for £180, he wore a dummy set. A Canadian had owned them for twenty years and they came on the market in 1965. They were offered to the Middlesex Regiment but the Regiment could not afford the asking price. However they asked to be informed where the medals went. This did not happen and Major Harold Couch of the "Die-Hards" noticed that they

F. J. Edwards' V.C. (Soldier)

that the bidding could go up to. The response was a very generous one and Messrs Baldwins were instructed to bid for the set at Glendining's Auction Rooms on October 26th 1966. The medals were knocked down to the Middlesex Regiment for £900. In addition to the V.C. which by this time of its chequered career was in a pretty battered state, the other medals were the 1914-15 Star, the British War Medal and the Victory Medal.

Edwards was a strong supporter of the various commemorative functions organised for the V.C. and G.C. holders but could neither read nor write. He was a 'mercurial, colourful character. . . and loved a fight with or without gloves.' At the time of his death his life long friend Bob Ryder described him as "my mad friend Patsy".

Gallahers Cigarette Card

Robert Edward Ryder was born at Harefield, Middlesex on December 17th 1895. He was educated at the Old Council School before finding work as a labourer. He enlisted with the 12th Middlesex (Duke of Cambridge's Own) in 1914. Six weeks before he left for France his wife died tragically early of consumption which she had contracted through asbestos dust when working at a gasmask factory. After his award for the V.C. was published he received a letter from the Brigadier-General of the 12th Middlesex and also from his platoon officer W. E. Inskip-Read who wrote:

"My Dear Ryder,

My most heartiest congratulations. I am not surprised to hear you have won the

Richmond Cemetery (D. C. Jennings)

Thiepval September 26th 1916

V.C. as I have always had a very high
opinion of you and knew, if ever you had
the opportunity, you would rise to the
occasion. Your wife and family have
good reason to be proud of you."

After the Somme battle was over and
two days after he was given his V.C. by
the King, Ryder was severely wounded in
the hip and was also peppered with
shrapnel splinters. The date was about
December lst 1916 and the next thing that
he was aware of, having lost conscious-
ness, was that he was in Hospital in
Norwich. He was out of action for some
time but asked to be returned to the fray
and subsequently fought on the Italian
Front and went on to win the Italian
Bronze Medal for swimming across the
River Piave under the eyes of the enemy
in order to rescue some troops who were
under heavy fire. This was in 1917.

R. E. Ryder with his father, Harefield

R. E. Ryder (Middlesex Regt.)

Ryder said that he needed his wife to go with him as his wounds gave him trouble and he needed assistance with dressing etc. He said that he would not go unless the Government paid, although the British Legion and the Middlesex Regiment both said that they would pay for his

At Edwards' funeral March 17th 1964

After the war he found employment difficult and in 1939 he quickly rejoined the Army, this time he became a sergeant instructor with the Royal Sussex Regiment. He was demobilized in Uxbridge and on coming out of the centre stopped two galloping horses who were careering down the main street at a time when children were coming out of school.

He farmed in New Brunswick, Canada until 1965 and then returned to England where he lived in Enfield, Middlesex. It was at this time that it was discovered that a piece of shrapnel was still lodged in his left leg. In 1966 he was one of 12 V.C. holders who were invited by the Government to attend the 50th anniversary of the battle of the Somme at Thiepval, France. Their expenses were to be paid; however wife's expenses. The problem must have been resolved as the smiling face of Bob Ryder in 1966 can be seen in some of the accompanying illustrations. In 1970 he moved from Albuhera Close, Enfield to Hucknall, Nottinghamshire. His second wife, Edna was a Hucknall woman. They had had six children, three boys and three girls. Two of the boys had served with the Middlesex Regiment at some time, and one with the Buckinghamshire Constabulary.

For a time Ryder worked at a local ordnance factory at Chilwell and it was at this period that his health began to fail, a contributory factor to his ill health was his war wounds. He fought for greater pensions for V.C. holders and having lost this battle he was 'too proud' to claim

St Marys Harefield (G. Gliddon)

social security. In May 1978 Mr Alf Morris, Minister for the Disabled visited Ryder, then aged 82 at his home in Annesley Road, Hucknall. In 1976 he had been invited to Buckingham Palace with other holders of the Victoria Cross and was greeted as Bob by Prince Philip. In 1977 he received the Queen's Jubilee Medal.

After having been a patient at Nottingham General Hospital, Ryder died at his home on December lst 1978, he was 82 years of age. Although the Ryders had been hard up they had refused to either sell the medals or to claim social security, Bob had expressed a wish to be buried in Harefield, his birthplace. He had put aside enough money for this eventuality and was given a military funeral at St Marys, Harefield. A childhood hero of Ryder's and another V.C. holder Major Gerald Goodlake was also buried in the same cemetery. The funeral took place on December 11th and buglers were supplied from the Queen's Divisional Depot as well as seven men who acted as pall bearers. A Nottingham firm offered to gild a wooden cross for Ryder's site but a standard Commonwealth War Grave Stone now marks the grave. There is a single inscription under his name and it is 'A Diehard', taken from the Middlesex Regimental Nickname. Ryder is also commemorated at the Guildhall, Westminster.

Although it was possible that Ryder in saving his companions at Thiepval on September 26th 1916 had killed over 100 Germans, he later reflected "I don't know why I did it. . . Normally I wouldn't hurt a fly." On his death the *Sunday Express* descibed him "as a shy but proud V.C." In 1979 news got out that Mrs Ryder was hard up, as she only had a pension and a small allowance to live on, and still steadfastly refused to sell her husband's medals which could have fetched £12,000. Edna had to appeal to people to stop sending her money, she had been sent over £600 from well wishers all over the country and had no way of returning it as most of the donations were sent anonymously.

In 1980 when she was 84 Edna gave her late husband's medals to the Imperial War Museum and at the opening of a special V.C. Exhibition was introduced to Prince Charles. Bob Ryder's medals formed part of the display.

T. E. Adlam

Gallahers Cigarette Card

F. J. Edwards and R. E. Ryder of the 12th Middlesex (54th Bde.) 18th (Eastern) Div. were not to be the only members of the 54th Bde, to win the V.C. during the struggle to capture Thiepval. They were joined by 2nd Lt. T. E. Adlam of the 7th Beds.

It will be remembered that the 54th Bde had made considerable progress in the attempt to capture the German stronghold on the 26th. On the 27th the Brigade arranged for the 7th Beds. who were in reserve in Thiepval Wood, to take over the front from the other three battalions, the 12th Middlesex, 11. R. Fus., and 6th Northants. This was to be done by 7 a.m. and the Beds. accompanied by the l/5th West Yorks. (146 Bde.) were to attack the final objective at a later hour. However when it was seen just how exposed the front line troops were, the relieving battalions were given the less arduous task of capturing the north-western part of Thiepval. The relief went well despite the darkness and the unfamiliarity of the featureless landscape. The attacking troops were in position at 5.45 a.m. They moved forward using bomb and bayonet and considered that not using artillery support was the best plan. Great progress was made on the left but a German machine gun held up the attack on the right flank. However 2nd. Lt Adlam, a considerable bomb thrower led a rush across the open ground and wiped out the machine gun crew. In doing so he was badly wounded in the leg. By 11 a.m. the Beds. were consolidating their positions to the north of the village. Seventy six prisoners had been captured, and the Bedfords had suffered ninety eight casualties. After dark the l/5th West

Receiving gold watch from the Mayor of Salisbury

this purpose also collected many enemy grenades. At this stage he was wounded in the leg, but nevertheless he was able to out-throw the enemy and then seizing his opportunity, and in spite of his wound, he led a rush, captured the position and killed the occupants. Throughout the day he continued to lead his men in bombing attacks.

On the following day he again displayed courage of the highest order, and though again wounded and unable to throw bombs, he continued to lead his men.

His magnificent example and valour, coupled with skilful handling of the situation, produced far-reaching results."

Adlam had been in the trenches for only two months and was 22 years of age.

Yorks. came up in support. On the next day Schwaben Redoubt finally fell but not before Stuff Redoubt was attacked first. The Bedfords had all their companies committed on this occasion and Adlam was wounded for a second time. Casualties on this occasion came to 122 killed or wounded. The 54th Bde. were then relieved.

Adlam's citation was published on November 24th 1916 and read as follows:

"For most conspicuous bravery during operations.

A portion of a village which had defied capture on the previous day had to be captured at all costs to permit subsequent operations to develop.

This minor operation came under very heavy machine gun and rifle fire.

Second Lieutenant Adlam realising that time was all important, rushed from shell hole to shell hole under heavy fire collecting men for a sudden rush, and for

Adlam in the 1930s

His ability to out-throw the German bombers was acquired at School where he had been known to throw a cricket ball as far as a 100 yards. His party had gathered up as many German bombs as they could find on the battle field and began a whirlwind attack on the enemy with these. In order to improve his throwing aim Adlam pulled off his equipment to allow him to throw better. It is likely that the speed of this attack totally stunned the German troops and when he led his men forward they had little trouble in killing or capturing their assailants. They had reached their first objective by 8.30 a.m. before moving on another 300 yards. By 11 a.m. the north west corner of Thiepval Village was in Allied hands and General Maxse of the 18th Division singled out Adlam for special praise and thanks. The next day Adlam continued to lead his men into action with no sense of danger to himself at the successful fight for the Schwaben Redoubt but as his right arm was wounded this time he was unable to throw bombs anymore.

Lt. Col. Frank Maxwell (Middlesex) in his letters wrote:

"This morning (27th) I had orders to clear out on relief by another regiment, but, much to the C.O.'s delight, I disobeyed the order and stayed on to see him through his attack on the stronghold that had beat us till then. I was in no mind to lose what we had so hardly won by going before he had done his job. And we only did it after three hours' attempt. But I have paid the penalty of a dressing down-by the General, who is furious. . ."

It is very clear from Maxwell's letters that he was genuinely surprised that the Brigade has done so well in such an exposed situation against troops who had known the ground for over a year.

School House, Blackmoor (D. A. B. Shardlow)

Adlam on the extreme right with five other V.C.s
June 1966 (Sunday Times)

Adlam was presented with his V.C. by the King at Buckingham Palace on December 2nd 1916. Because of his wounds sustained at Thiepval on September 27th/28th Adlam was taken off infantry duties and transferred to the Army Educational Corps.

Thomas Edwin Adlam was the son of John Adlam and Evangeline Adlam and was born in Waterloo Gardens, Salisbury on October 21st 1893. He was educated at Bishop Wordworth's School in Salisbury and trained to be a teacher in Basingstoke. He joined the Territorial Force in 1912 and on November 16th 1915 was given a commission as a Second Lieutenant. Between April 1916 and January 1919 he served as an Instructor at No 2 Officer Cadet Bn., Cambridge. There

must have been at least a two or three month break in these duties when he served with the infantry on the Western Front. On June 21st he married Ivy Annete, daughter of Mr and Mrs W. H. Mace of Farnborough, Hants. The ceremony took place at St Marys Church, South Farnborough. His address was Lynchford House, Farnborough.

Adlam was demobilized on November 15th 1919 but for a time remained with the Army and served in Ireland at the time of "The Troubles." He then officially retired in March 1923. and his address at this time was Guildford House, South Farnborough. He was made the headmaster of Blackmoor C. E. school at Blackmoor, Liss. He had become known as the "Salisbury" V.C. and in the 1920s was presented with a gold watch by the Mayor as well as being invited to unveil the city's war memorial. He had also continued to be on the Officers Reserve List and two weeks before the Second War broke out in 1939 Adlam was recalled to the Colours. He enlisted with the Royal Engineers which took him to Avonmouth Docks and then he became Deputy Assistant Quarter Master General at Glasgow, Dover and Tilbury where he was serving at the time of the D. Day landings in June 1944.

Adlam ended the war as a Lt. Colonel and returned to his school at Blackmoor. His family had grown to four children and when his school was closed he bought it for his family and converted it into a house. He retired early and did a number of different jobs and especially enjoyed his work on the Woolmer Estate of Lord Selborne. In 1966 he was one of a group of V.C. holders who were invited by the Ministry of Defence to take part in the 50th anniversary commemoration of the Battle of the Somme at Thiepval. Tom Adlam always regarded himself as a schoolmaster first and as a soldier second. He was a keen gardener and cricketer, he kept wicket for a local team until the age of 71. He died at Hayling Island on May 28th 1975 while on holiday with one of his daughters. He was 81 years of age and was buried at St. Matthews, Blackmoor, across the road from where he used to live, in a grave that he shares with his wife.

Blackmoor Cemetery (D. A. B. Shardlow)

When he was questioned about his gallantry on the Somme Adlam was like many V.C. holders, reticent on the matter. He often made the point that "others had suffered and had nothing to show for their efforts and that thousands had died doing what he had done and he was always conscious of the terrible price that his comrades had paid in those battles of 1916."

Adlam's V.C. was kept in a bank vault for many years for safety but in 1990 his family presented it on loan to Luton Museum as part of their Royal Anglian Regimental display.

A. C. T. White

The battle for possession of the Thiepval Ridge continued to October lst when Stuff Redoubt was consolidated and most of the Schwaben Redoubt was taken.

Stuff Redoubt was one of several German redoubts to the north of Mou-

quet Farm and to the north east of Thiepval. It was north west of Zollern Redoubt and due east of the Schwaben. Pozieres was to the east and Grandcourt to the west.

On September 28th the 32nd Bde of

Gallahers Cigarette Card

advance owing to the German barrage and congestion in the trenches. However the party of the two other Yorkshire battalions under the leadership of Captain A. C. T. White (Green Howards) did have some success later on in the evening. They managed to bomb their way forward and were able to capture most of Stuff Redoubt's northern face. However they were not able to hang on to what they had taken, as they lacked both the men and ammunition. Despite this they somehow clung on to the positions that they had gained.

On September 30th Captain White was once again in the thick of the fighting and led his group of Yorkshiremen in the attack from the southern face of Stuff Redoubt. Convergent bombing attacks were made and a party of the 6th Y&L (32nd Bde.) moved along eastwards from Hessian Trench and the 7th S. Staffs. (33rd Bde.) moved up the Zollern Trench. The joint attack worked and before darkness fell the 11th Div. were in control of all of its objectives except for the northern half of the redoubt. The 11th Div. were relieved by the 25th Div. and

the 11th Div. was supposed to capture Stuff Redoubt and then link up with the Canadian Army's left flank by capturing Hessian Trench which ran eastwards from Stuff. Two companies of the 8th D.W.R. (32nd Bde.) were positioned in Zollern Trench, ready for the assault and a mixture of men from the 9th West Yorks. and 6th Green Howards who were holding on to their positions in Stuff Redoubt, were meant to complete its capture.

When zero hour of 6 p.m. arrived the 8th D.W.R. found that they could not

Stuff Redoubt October 1st 1916

the Green Howards moved to hutments at Varennes, south of Acheux.

Captain White was awarded the V.C. for his leadership in the period of fighting for Stuff Redoubt between September 27th and October lst. The citation was published on October 26th 1916 and read as follows:

"For most conspicuous bravery. He was in command of the troops that held the southern and western faces of a redoubt. For four days and nights, by his indomitable spirit, great personal courage, and skilful dispositions, he held his position under fire of all kinds and against several counter-attacks. Though short of supplies and ammunition, his determination never wavered. When the enemy attacked in greatly superior numbers and had almost ejected our troops from the redoubt, he personally led a counter-attack, which finally cleared the enemy out of the southern and western faces. He risked his life continually and was the life and soul of the defence."

Captain White was presented with his V.C. by the King at Hyde Park, London on June 2nd 1917. He was the fourth member of the Green Howards to win the V.C. in the Somme battle, a record for the battalions taking part.

Archie Cecil Thomas White was born at Boroughbridge, Yorkshire on October 5th 1890. He was one of two sons of Mr and Mrs Thomas White who lived at

Norwood House, Langthorpe, Borough-bridge. Thomas White was an outfitter. The ancient Yorkshire market town had at one time sent two Members of Parliament to Westminster.

A. C. T. White (Green Howards)

White was educated at Harrogate Grammar School and King's College, London and became one of its Fellows. He enlisted with the Yorkshire Regiment (Green Howards) and became a Second Lieutenant in 1914. He served at Gallipoli with the 6th Green Howards at Suvla Bay in 1915 and a severe attack of dysentery probably saved his life as he could not take part in an attack in which almost all the officers were killed. His brother, John Finlayson however who had enlisted as a Private and then became an officer with the same batta-

lion was to die of wounds in the same campaign. Archie White himself was wounded in the Dardanelles and was later transferred to France with the 6th Green Howards and gained the M.C. before his V.C. at Stuff Redoubt. He was to write of his experience 50 years later in 1966 and said that:

"When after 48 hours a message got through from Corps H.Q. asking how long we could hold on, being a very bumptious person I replied 'Till the cows come home'."

After the Somme battle White became a Bde. Major of the staff of another Somme V.C. holder Brigadier General J. V. Campbell of the Coldstream Guards. White found him a difficult man to serve and he had already got through three of four Brigade Majors before White's appearance. Despite early misgivings the two men did hit it off and in time also became good friends. White later served as a Bde. Major with the Archangel Relief Force in North Russia.

After the war he decided to join the Army Educational Corps as a junior Major and by then had married and his family consisted of two daughters, with one to be born later. At the time he was the youngest Major in the British Army. He held appointments at Sandhurst, and in India and Burma. He became Command Education Officer in the Northern, and later Southern A. A. Commands. On the formation of 21 Army Group, he was appointed its chief education officer and served with the British Army of Liberation throughout north west Europe in the Second War. After further service in south east Asia he retired in 1947, after 33 years in the Army, he had reached the rank of Colonel in 1942. He became the Principal of the City Literary Institute in London between 1948 and 1956. The

Thiepval Memorial July 1966. Left to right Rev. A. Proctor, R. E. Ryder, J. Hutchinson,
A. C. T. White, T. Adlam and T. Veale (Soldier)

Institute had 10,000 adult part time students and a wide ranging syllabus. Although he had retired from the position of head he returned to give classes on retirement. He then became a member of the Senate of the University of London and served on various other educational committees. When Sir Hugh Stockwell became Colonel commandant of the Royal Army Educational Corps and was also appointed to Supreme Headquarters, Allied Powers in Europe, White became deputy Colonel commandant.

In 1963 White published a book on the history of Army Education. In 1966 he was one of 12 V.C. Holders invited by the Ministry of Defence to take part at the 50th anniversary commemoration ceremonies of the Battle of the Somme at Thiepval. He was then 65 years of age and still looked a very upright and distinguished English gentleman. He was a man of Christian beliefs and a great supporter of his former regiment, the Green Howards. He was also a prominent member of the Victoria and George Cross Association. He died at his home, Brucklay, Upper Park Road, Camberley on May 20th 1971 at the age of 80. His wife had died in 1960. He was cremated at Woking Crematorium and his name is listed in Bay (19/173). His medals are in the possession of the the Green Howards Museum, Richmond, North Yorkshire.

R. B. Bradford

R. B. Bradford

As a continuation for the battle for possession of the Transloy Ridges the plan for October 1st 1916 was for the Fourth Army to capture Eaucourt l'Abbaye and the Flers line as far as Le Sars. The l'Abbaye consisted of two large farms built on the site of an Augustine abbey that were in the same enclosure. The Flers line at the end of September ran in a south easterly direction from the south of this position to the south west of Flers.

The New Zealand 2nd Bde. were on the right in a line that stretched from Flers Trench to Gird Trench; on their left was the 47th London Div. and on their left was the 151st Bde. of the 50th (Northumbrian) Div. We are concerned

here with this last named unit which contained four battalions; the l/5th Borders, and three battalions of the Durham Light Infantry, the l/6th, l/8th and l/9th. The l/6th was in fact on October 1st a composite battalion made up from men of the l/5th Borders, the l/8th Durhams, and the l/5th Northd. Fus. from the 149th Bde.

In the fighting the right flank of the l/6th Durhams became exposed by the failure of the 47th Div.'s left flank, which had been caught very badly by enemy machine gunners. The Durhams were able to cling on to a weak position in Flers Trench. Major G. E. Wilkinson commander of the l/6th Durhams was severely wounded in the arm and retired from the action and sought out Lt. Col. Roland Bradford, commanding officer of the l/9th Durhams who were in support to the attacking battalions. Bradford was in his headquarters position called Seven Elms, about half a mile in front of High

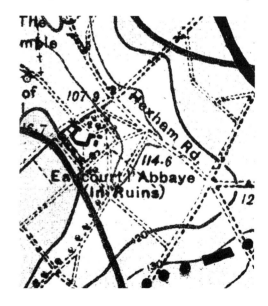

Eaucourt l'Abbaye October 1st 1916

Wood. Wilkinson told Bradford of the situation and suggested to him that he should assume command of the l/6th in addition to the l/9th and to go up the line and take charge of what was a precarious situation. Wilkinson had no suitable senior officer on his staff, only junior officers.

As a result of Bradford taking control of the two battalions Flers Trench was captured by 9.30 p. m. Bradford was later to be awarded the V.C. for his inspired leadership and organising ability on this occasion. He was first recommended for the D.S.O. by Brig. Gen Cameron of the 151st Bde. but as more details of his action came through, this was changed to the V.C.

Unfortunately while Bradford was winning his V.C. another recipient Sgt.

D. F. Brown of the 2nd Otagos was losing his life. Brown would not have been aware that he had gained a V.C. in the fighting on September 15th and when he was killed he was carrying out a very similar act. He rushed a German machine gun position single handed and was killed soon afterwards at a former German position called The Circus which was north east of Eaucourt l'Abbaye.

Bradford's citation was published on November 25th 1916 and read as follows:

"For most conspicuous bravery and good leadership in attack, whereby he saved the situation on the right flank of his Brigade and of the Division.

Lt. Col.'s Bradford's battalion was in support. A leading battalion having suffered very severe casualties, and the commander having been wounded, its flank became dangerously exposed at close quarters to the enemy. Raked by machine-gun fire, the situation of the battalion was critical. At the request of the wounded Commander, Lt. Col. Bradford asked permission to command the exposed battalion in addition to his own.

Permission granted, he at once proceeded to the foremost lines.

By his fearless energy under fire of all description, and his skilful leadership of the two Battalions, regardless of all danger, he succeeded in rallying the attack, captured and defended the objectives, and so secured the flank."

It is unlikely that Bradford waited for permission from Brigadier Cameron be-fore taking charge as Wilkinson did not inform the Brigadier until reaching Bde. H.Q. which was two miles behind the lines. There would have been no time to lose as the situation was so critical on the right flank of the attack.

On November 5th the 151st Bde. of the 50th Div. were again in the thick of the action, this time in an attack against the Butte de Warlencourt a small hillock to the north west of Eaucourt l'Abbaye. The Australians were to the right and the 46th Div. to the left. The objectives were the Butte itself and a quarry to the south west close to the Bapaume road. The Gird position was also to be consolidated. The attack which was an impossible one

Hyde Park June 2nd 1917. From left to right: T. Hughes, J. Cunningham, A. C. T. White, R. B. Bradford, F. W. Palmer and W. B. Allen

Carwood House, Witton Park, Bishop Auckland (Jack Cavanagh)

for the Durham battalions to succeed with failed although small parties of the Durhams did actually reach the Butte itself before German counter attacks removed them. The attacking troops had been enfiladed by machine gun fire from both flanks and the ground was so muddy and the position so exposed that there was no chance of a victory. Indeed Bradford was doubtful of the value of the capture of the small hill, however he did note that it "had become an obsession. Everybody wanted it." Bradford received his V.C. from the King at Hyde Park on June 2nd 1917, he was the 14th person out of 350 to receive an award from the King and the number 13 had been left out of the programme.

Roland Boys Bradford was born on February 23rd 1892 at Witton Park, Bishop Auckland. He was the fourth of five sons of George and Amy Bradford of Carr House, Witton Park. George Bradford was a colliery manager. Roland was baptised at St Paul's Church, Witton Park by the Revd. Charles Aubrey on March 23rd 1892. He was educated at the Royal Naval School, Eltham and Epsom College. He entered the Army from the Territorial Force in May 1912 before receiving a commission with the Durham Light Infantry. He had become a keen horseman and was fond of competitive sports.

At the beginning of the war in 1914 Roland Bradford embarked with the 2nd D.L.I. and they landed at St. Nazaire on September 10th 1914. He was made a Lieutenant on September 25th and was eventually to become a Brigadier General. Eight months later in May 1915 Bradford became the Adjutant with the 7th D.L.I. and he held this position until

St Pauls Witton Park, Bishop Auckland (Jack Cavanagh)

Hermies British Cemetery (C.W.G.C.)

early in 1916 when he acted as Bde. Major. In May 1916 he became commanding officer of the 9th D.L.I., a battalion with whom he was to remain until November 1917. He then became the youngest Brigadier-General in the British Army and took over command of the 186th Bde. of the 62nd (West Riding.) Div. He was 25 years of age, and only had a few weeks to live. He was involved in the attack on the Hindenburg line and was killed by a stray shell that hit his Brigade H.Q., near Graincourt, on November 30th. He was buried at Hermies British Cemetery Row F, Grave 10. His name is commemorated at St. Pauls, Witton Park with the Rose Window, situated high up on the west wall of the church. His brother G. N. Bradford, a Lt. Commander in the Royal Navy also won the V.C. (posthumously) during the attack on the Mole, Zeebrugge, Belgium on St. George's Day, April 23rd 1918. A third brother who also died was James Barker Bradford of the 18th D.L.I. who died of wounds in May 1917. Captain Thomas A. Bradford, later Sir Thomas was awarded the D.S.O. and survived the war, he lived in Darlington. Amy the boys' mother used to place an 'In Memoriam' notice in *The Times* every

Hermies British Cemetery (D. C. Jennings)

anniversary of the deaths of her three sons. She herself died in January 1951 in Folkestone.

Roland who was obviously a born soldier was also awarded the M.C. in addition to the V.C. and his medals are in the possession of the Museum of the Durham Light Infantry.

H. Kelly

On October 2nd 1916 the Germans counter attacked the Eaucourt position and the British failed to hold onto the village of Le Sars. The British recovered Eaucourt l'Abbaye the next day and on the 4th, 2nd Lt. H. Kelly was to win the V.C for extreme bravery during an attack against Le Sars.

Flers Support Trench naturally ran alongside Flers Trench and they both went in a south easterly direction of

the German held village of Le Sars, in front of Eaucourt l'Abbaye towards Flers. The two divisions involved in the fight for Le Sars were the 47th to the right and the 23rd to the left. On October 4th the 47th Div. captured the rest of Flers Support without much opposition and then pushed on towards a position to the north west of Eaucourt l'Abbaye. The 23rd Div., to the left of the 47th endeavoured to carry the section of Flers

Gallahers Cigarette Card

Support to the north of the Bapaume
Road. The 10th D.W.R. (69th Bde.)
relieved the 8th K.O.Y.L.I. (70th Bde.)
23rd Div. on the afternoon of the 2nd of
October. The relief was very much
delayed owing to congestion in the
trenches and was not completed until
dawn on the 3rd. *The Iron Duke* which is
the journal of the Duke of Wellington's
Regiment (Vol. VIII No 23 October 1932)
suggests that the action for which Kelly
was decorated actually took place on the
3rd and not on the 4th of October. The
journal says the action took place as part
of a "small operation, preliminary to the

battle of Le Sars, . . ." The history of the
23rd Division by Lt. Col. H. R. Sandi-
lands described the situation as follows:

"But as a preliminary to this big attack
the G.O.C. 69th Bde. determined to
endeavour to improve his position by two
small operations, designed to capture the
portion of Flers 2 still held by the enemy,
and a short length of Flers 1 to the south
of the Bapaume Road, in which the
enemy had again obtained a footing.

On the evening of October 3rd,
following artillery preparations, two
small companies of the 10th Duke of
Wellington's attacked Flers 2 north of the
Bapaume Road, while a party of the 8th
Yorkshire Regiment carried out a simul-
taneous bombing attack against the
enemy in Flers 1.

To gain their objective, the Duke of
Wellington's had but 100 yards to cross.
But their advance lay across mud and
mire of the most appalling description,
and was met by a withering fire of rifles
and machine guns. Following their lead-
ers, among whom 2nd Lts. Stafford,
Harris and Kelly were conspicuous in the
example they set, the men pushed

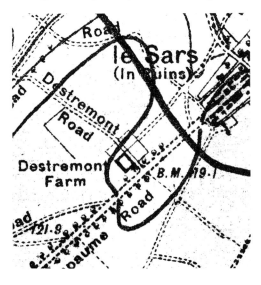

forward with the greatest gallantry, and gained the enemy's wire. Here they were held up. To cross a greater distance in these conditions would have been scarcely possible, but the distance of the assembly trenches from the objective had been insufficient to enable the artillery to deal effectively with the wire. Stafford and Harris were killed, and the attack broke down."

Henry Harris and Henry Stafford are both listed in *Officers Died in the Great War* as having been killed on October 4th.

The citation for Kelly's V.C. was published on November 25th and read as follows:

"For most conspicuous bravery in attack.

He twice rallied his Company under

H. Kelly

the heaviest fire, and finally led the only three available men into the enemy trench, and there remained bombing until two of them had become casualties and enemy reinforcements had arrived.

He then carried his Company Serjeant-Major, who had been wounded, back to our trenches, a distance of 70 yards, and subsequently three other soldiers.

He set a fine example of gallantry and endurance."

Kelly was presented with his V.C. by the King at Buckingham Palace on February 14th 1917.

———

Henry Kelly was born at Rochdale Road, Manchester on July 10th 1887. He was the eldest of a family of ten children to be born to Charles Kelly of Dublin and Jane (formerly McGarry) of Manchester. He went to St Patrick's School Manchester, and the Xaverian Brothers College, Victoria Park, Manchester. His father died in 1904 and Henry was left as head of the family and became a sorting clerk at Newton Street Post Office in Manchester. He trained with the Manchester Royal Engineers Territorials and later left his home in King Street, Moston, Manchester and enlisted in the Cameron Highlanders as a Private on September 5th 1914, he was 27 years of age. He transferred to the Manchester Regiment and gained his first stripe before becoming a Sgt. Major two weeks later. He was commissioned on May 12th 1915 into the 10th Duke of Wellington's and went overseas to France in the same month. On September 11th 1916 he was made a Temporary Lieutenant. After he had won the V.C. in October 1916 his Corps Commander decorated him with the ribbon of the V.C.

In 1917 he was present at the battle for Messines Ridge (June 6th 1917) and at the Menin Road in September as part of the Third Battle of Ypres and was made a Temporary Captain on September 21st. In 1918 he was involved in the fighting in Italy at the Asiago Plateau and gained a M.C. for his role in a raid on the enemy trenches during the night of June 21st/22nd. A large number of the enemy were killed. A few months later he gained a bar to his M.C. in an attack on the Austrian positions across the Piave on October 27th where again his leadership resulted in the capturing of many prisoners and the capture of enemy machine guns.

By the end of the war Kelly was to become one of the most decorated officers of the war and in addition to gaining the V.C. and two M.C.s he was also awarded the Belgian Croix de Guerre and the French Military Medal. He left the Army in January 1920 after having been promoted to the rank of Temporary Major and put in charge of a Rest Camp in France.

After the war he returned to work for the Post Office but in 1936 went to Spain to take part in the Spanish Civil War. He was awarded yet another medal which was the Grand Laurelled Cross of San Fernando. When the Second War began

Kelly served as a Lieutenant in the Cheshire Regiment and from October 1943 to February 1944 he was in charge of the District Claims office of the London District at Curzon Street. Unfortunately and probably owing to the pressure of work at the time he allegedly made fraudulent claims for travel expenses, to the value of two pounds, ten shillings. He was court-martialled and severely reprimanded. He resigned his commission and rejoined the Post Office in 1944. He lived at 178 Hall Lane, Baguley, Wythenshawe, with his wife Kathleen and two children.

Kelly died after a long illness at Prestwich Hospital, Manchester on January 18th 1960. He was given a private funeral which was attended by representitives of his old regiment as well as members of his family. He was buried in a grave without a memorial stone which is numbered 1/372 at the Southern Cemetery, Manchester.

Kelly's medals are in the keeping of the Duke of Wellington's Regiment, Halifax. It is to be hoped that Henry Kelly will be remembered as an outstanding soldier and also as one of the most decorated officers in the Great War.

J. C. Richardson

In the four days that elapsed between Lt. H. Kelly winning his V.C. at Le Sars and the 8th of October when Piper Richardson was to win his, there had been slight progress in the battle. The British had advanced to the north west of Eaucourt and the French had made progress to the north east of Morval. On the 8th the 1st Canadian Division were to advance to The Quadrilateral on the Le Sars Line, which was to the north west of the village itself and also reach Regina Trench which

ran across their lines in a south westerly direction. Regina ran from the north of Courcelette to Stuff Trench which in turn joined the Schwaben Redoubt.

The attack began at 4.50 a.m. on the 8th when it was still dark and also raining. The two Canadian Bdes. under the leadership of Major-General Currie were the 1st on the right and the 3rd on the left. The 3rd and 4th Battalions of the 1st Bde. attacked the right hand objectives, the Le Sars Line and The Quadrilateral. They

J. C. Richardson (Canadian Archive)

back the 16th found that it could not hang on. The Royal Highlanders on the left were also held up by uncut wire, and after suffering heavy casualties fell back before dark. It seems that the uncut wire was a huge problem all along the line, and one can only assume that the artillery should either have been more destructive of the wire or that over optimistic reports allowed the attack to take place. In addition the Canadian lines were crescent shaped and the Germans had a concave front on this sector which gave them a distinct advantage over their Canadian attackers.

However we are concerned here with the role of the 16th Bn. and in particular of Piper James Cleland Richardson. To quote the diary of the battalion:

"When our barrage started," said Company Sergeant-Major Mackie, who was advancing on the left flank of the leading wave Number 4 Company, "Major Lynch, Captain Bell, Piper Richardson and myself went out of the trench. After waiting for five minutes we bade goodbye to Captain Bell who was to take over the second line of the Company, and

reached the former but owing to uncut wire were held up at the second and also had to swerve to the left when looking for gaps in the uncut wire. The two battalions therefore mingled together on the left. In the afternoon a threatened German counter attack was delayed by the intervention of the artillery but the Canadians were forced back, being greatly out-numbered and also out of bombs. They ended the day at their jumping-off trenches.

On the left of 1st Canadian Bde was the 16th Bn. (Canadian) Scottish and the 13th Bn. (R. Highlanders) and the former battalion did enter Regina Trench after forcing its way through the wire. However as the 3rd Bn. on its right fell

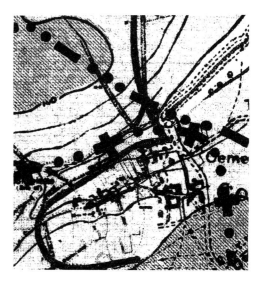

Major Lynch gave the order to advance. The three of us walked in front of the leading line; Piper Richardson on the Major's left and I on his right. The going was easy as the ground was not cut up. About half-way over I commenced to wonder why the piper wasn't playing and crossed over by the side of him to ask the reason. He said he had been told not to play until ordered to do so by the Major."

The party reached the wire which they found to be uncut and when they were searching for an opening the Germans began to throw bombs and opened rifle fire, Major Lynch fell mortally wounded. Richardson asked Mackie if he could play his pipes and was told to go ahead. The wire still slowed down the Canadian advance and many men from the first two waves became casualties because of the intense fire. Richardson according to eye witnesses walked up and down in front of the wire for fully ten minutes thereby inspiring about a hundred men of the Canadian/Scottish battalions to greater effort in their attack against Regina Trench. Richardson must have been leading a charmed life and he also helped with the bombing attack against the enemy. He later helped a wounded colleague back to safety and on realising that he had mislaid his pipes, he went back to recover them. He was never seen alive again, although his body was recovered from the battlefield.

Richardson's gallantry on October 8th/9th 1916 inspired a great deal of publicity and presumably because of the image of the lone piper walking up and down in no man's land under intense fire but seemingly untouched by it all. Much of this publicity was written up for reasons of propaganda and was of a *Boys Own Paper* type. As late as September 1965 a comic strip version of Richardson's bravery was published in a magazine called *The Victor*.

Richardson's posthumous award was not announced, owing to some administrative delay until October 22nd 1918 and read as follows:

"For most conspicuous bravery and devotion to duty when, prior to attack, he obtained permission from his Commanding Officer to play his company "over the top."

As the company approached the objective it was held up by very strong wire and came under intense fire, which caused heavy casualties and demoralised the formation for the moment. Realising the situation, Piper Richardson strode up and down outside the wire, playing his pipes with the greatest coolness. The effect was instantaneous. Inspired by his splendid example, the company rushed the wire with such fury and determination that the obstacle was overcome and the position captured.

Later, after participating in bombing operations, he was detailed to take back a wounded comrade and prisoners.

After proceeding about 200 yards Piper Richardson remembered that he had left his pipes behind. Although strongly urged not to do so, he insisted on returning to recover his pipes. He has never been seen since and death has been presumed accordingly owing to lapse of time."

James Cleland Richardson was born at Bellshill, Lanarkshire, Scotland on November 25th 1895. He was the son of David Richardson and Mary Prosser Richardson and went to school at Bellshill Academy, Auchwraith Public School, Blantyre and John Street Public School, Bridgeton, Glasgow. His family moved to Canada a few years before the

The Victor, September 4th 1965

Adanac Military Cemetery (C.W.G.C.)

war where his father became a Chief of Police in British Columbia.

James Richardson joined the Canadian Forces at the outbreak of war in August 1914 when he was 18 years of age, his unit was the 72nd Seaforth Highlanders. When he went to France with the Canadian Forces he was attached to the 16th Canadian Scottish and was with them in the famous Canadian stand at St. Julien in April 1915. In 1916 it was Major C. W. Peck who recommended that Richardson should be awarded a posthumous V.C. Peck later became commander of the 16th Bn. (Canadian) Scottish and won a V.C. himself at Cagnicourt in early September 1918.

Richardson was buried at Adanac Military Cemetery, Plot 111, Row F, Grave 36. He was not yet 21 when he was killed. His medals were at one time in the hands of his sister Mrs Charles A. Murray

Adanac Military Cemetery (D. C. Jennings)

of Blackburn, White Rock, British Columbia and are still in private hands.

R. Downie

Gallahers Cigarette Card

artillery shelled the village and its cemetery and then changed to a creeping barrage behind which the attacking troops of the 11th Bde (4th Div.) advanced with the 1st Hampshires and the 2nd R. Dublins (10th Bde.) on the right flank. The former battalion together with the French (152nd Div.) were stopped almost at once by attacking fire from the trench called Boritska, which was the attackers' objective. They were also troubled by machine guns concealed in shell holes. When the 1st Rifle Bde. (11th Bde. 4th Div.) arrived to give assistance the advance progressed and positions were established north west of the objective. After darkness fell it was found that the Dubliners had captured the gun-pits, to the east of Lesboeufs and also a strongpoint beyond them. It was at this time that Sgt. R. Downie (2nd R. Dub. Fus.) gained the V.C.

It was said that after the Dubliners had lost their officers that Sgt. Downie took

Piper Richardson won his V.C. at Regina Trench on October 8th 1916 and the Allies did not make any substantial progress during the next fortnight. On October 23rd 1916 the Fourth Army planned to capture the German positions and to reach a position in front of Le Transloy from which the village could be assaulted. It was a misty morning and the operation was delayed in the hope that the visibility would improve. The Allied

immediate control and with the rallying cry of "Come on, the Dubs." rushed the German machine gun crew and scattered them. There was a determined series of counter attacks but Downie's men beat them off and established their defences. It was said that Downie was "everywhere, directing, counselling, and cheering on the men who he had led so bravely forward!"

The citation was published on November 25th 1916 and read as follows:

"For most conspicuous bravery and devotion to duty in attack.

When most of the officers had become casualties, this Non-Commissioned Officer, utterly regardless of personal danger moved about under heavy fire and reorganised the attack, which had been temporarily checked. At the critical moment he rushed forward alone, shouting, "Come on, the Dubs."

This stirring appeal met with immediate response, and the line rushed forward at his call.

Sergeant Downie accounted for several of the enemy, and in addition captured a machine gun, killing the team. Though wounded early in the fight, he remained with his company, and gave valuable assistance, while the position was being consolidated.

R. Downie in the 1930s

It was owing to Sergeant Downie's courage and initiative that this important position, which had resisted four or five previous attacks, was won."

Downie was given his V.C. by the King at York Cottage, Sandringham, Norfolk on January 8th 1917.

Robert Downie was born at Springburn Road, Glasgow on January 12th 1894. He was the son of Mr Francis Downie and

East of Lesboeufs October 23rd 1916

Mrs Elizabeth Jane Downie. Robert was one of 16 children, five of whom were to serve in the Great War with two of them being killed. He was educated at St. Aloysius's School, Springburn, and went to work at the Hydepark Locomotive Works, Glasgow where his father had worked for most of his life. On January 12th 1912 Robert joined the Army and went to France in August 1914, he was to be wounded five times before the war was over and this included being gassed. On April 4th 1914, he married Ivy Sparks at Gravesend, by the end of the war they had had three children, one of whom died in infancy.

A few days before the King was to give Downie his V.C. he returned home to Glasgow where he was given a public welcome at the Springburn Town Hall, Glasgow. In the evening he was given a special reception by the United Irish League and was given a gold watch by his former school and a purse containing treasury notes.

He left the Army in March 1919 and in addition to the V.C. he also gained the Military Medal and the Mons Medal, as well as the Russian Order of St. George. In addition he was mentioned in Despatches twice.

After the war he was an avid supporter of the various functions organised for holders of the V.C and G.C. and attended at least twelve of these occasions. In 1941 (July 29th) he attended the funeral of Lt. Henry May V.C. in Glasgow who was the first Glasgow man to win the V.C. in the Great War. Walter Ritchie another holder of a Somme V.C. also attended.

Downie himself died on April 18th 1968 at the age of 74, at the present time his medals are in private hands.

E. P. Bennett

There was a gap of thirteen days between Sgt. Downie winning his V.C. at Lesboeufs and Lt. E. P. Bennett winning his in the fighting for Le Transloy. Not a great deal of progress had been made by the Allies during this time on the Somme front and the reason was quite simple, it was rain. I calculate that about 41 mm of rain fell in this period which in turn made conditions for fighting well nigh impossible. The French made progress to the north west of Sailly-Saillisel and the British progressed slowly towards Le Transloy. On other fronts though the French had re-entered Vaux.

General Rawlinson commander of the Fourth Army had proposed to limit this attack planned for November 5th to the capture of ground to the east and north east of Lesboeufs. The French at the same time were planning to capture St. Pierre Vaast Wood, which when accomplished would create a dangerous salient which Lord Cavan (XIV Corps) undertook to cover.

The 33rd Div. were situated at Lesboeufs and consisted of the 19th, 98th and 100th Bdes. The 100th contained the 2nd Worcesters who we are concerned with here. On the 4th the 2nd R. Welch were ordered to dig trenches on the crest of the ridge in front of Le Transloy but little was achieved because of the open-ness of the position. The actual objective at Le Transloy was the cemetery and the enemy machine gunners were on the alert. The 2nd Worcesters made a flank attack from the French positions, to the right of the 33rd Div. and captured Boritska and Mirage Trenches and then

Gallahers Cigarette Card

little 2nd Lieutenant (possibly Jack Oswald Couldridge) struck dead. Still grasping the spade, he reached the troops, dashed through them and signalled them to advance. The whole Battalion rose behind him and flooded forward in one wave over the crest-line and down onto the flank of the German trenches."

This was when the German positions at Mirage and Boritzka trenches gave way. The Worcesters advanced down the slope towards Le Transloy for a distance of 500 yards and then dug in and consolidated their positions. They then linked up with the 16 K.R.R.C. The Worcesters were later relieved by the 5th Scottish Rifles. (19th Bde.) Bennett returned with a party of only 60 men to receive congratulations from Battalion H.Q. at Lesboeufs. The trench that they had occupied was later named Bennett's trench,

Bennett's citation was published on December 30th 1916 and read as follows:

"For most conspicuous bravery in action when in command of the second wave of the attack. Finding that the first wave had suffered heavy casualties, its commander killed and the line wavering,

joined up with the 16 K.R.R.C of the same brigade. The Worcesters' first wave had been unsuccessful and the leader of the second wave Lt. E. P. Bennett (C. Coy.) took over both units and urged the infantry on. He had recently been blown up by a shell and his wounds had been bandaged by a considerate Frenchman, and he carried on leading the advance with a spade in his hand. The regimental history describes the incident in the following manner:

"Lieutenant Bennett found a spade and cut himself a step in the embankment. Then he ran forward through the bursting shells. As he ran, he passed the

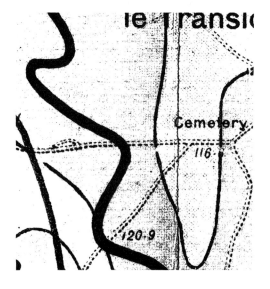

Le Transloy November 5th 1916

E. P. Bennett

Lt. Bennett advanced at the head of the second wave, and by his personal example of valour and resolution reached his objective with but sixty men.

Isolated with his small party, he at once took steps to consolidate his position under heavy rifle and machine gun fire from both flanks, and although wounded, he remained in command directing and controlling.

He set an example of cheerfulness and resolution beyond all praise, and there is little doubt that but for his personal example of courage, the attack would have been checked at the outset."

Bennett was decorated by the King on February 5th 1917 at Buckingham Palace and was the second man from the Worcester Regiment to gain the V.C. during the battle of the Somme.

PUBLIC RECEPTION
FEB. 21ST, 1917.

Illuminated Address (W. Oliver Wicks)

Eugene Paul Bennett was the fourth of
five sons of Mr Charles Bennett, a former
headmaster, and accountant and Florence Emma Sophia Bennett, there was
also a daughter, Dora. Paul was born at
Cainscross, Stroud, Gloucestershire on
June 4th 1892. He was educated at
Marling School, which was the local
grammar school in Stroud between 1905
and 1908. He was a good cricketer and
footballer. He later joined the staff of the
Bank of England. In October 1913 he
joined the Artists Rifles as a private and
went with the 1st Artists to France in
October 1914. He was given a commission with the 2nd Worcesters on January
1st 1915, and remained with them until
the day he gained his V.C. He was
present at the battle of Neuve Chapelle

and on September 26th he was awarded a
M.C. during the battle of Loos and was
mentioned in despatches. He received
the M.C. at Buckingham Palace from the
King on May 10th 1916. His parents
whose address was "Fromehurst", Frome
Park Road, Stroud were with their son at
the Ceremony. At the time that Bennett
was gaining his V.C. in November 1916
he had as we have seen been wounded
and he spent several months recovering.
On his discharge he was made a Captain
and was fit enough to return to Stroud
whose inhabitants were eager to give him
a special welcome which they arranged
for February 21st 1917. His train was met
by members of the Stroud Council as well
as by members of his family, and a guard
of honour was drawn up for inspection.
Banners of welcome draped the town's
streets and many shops and offices were
closed to allow their employees to greet
their 'local hero'. Bennett and his family

E. P. Bennett in the 1930s

18 Manor Gardens, S.W. 19 (D. Halsey)

were installed in a Rolls Royce which was drawn through the town to a platform where the welcoming ceremony was to take place. He was greeted on behalf of the town by the vice chairman of Stroud Urban District Council and presented with an Illuminated Address. Later that evening a dinner was given in his honour at the Holloway Institute and he gave a modest speech. His brother Theodore was allowed to attend the celebrations. On October 18th 1918 Bennett sustained very severe shell splinter wounds and was still confined to bed nearly a year later, which was the reason why he could not attend his father's funeral in September 1919. On his return to civilian life the bank presented him with a "sword of honour". Bennett had had three brothers one of whom Lt. Harold R. G. A. was

killed in a motor cycle accident; another was Lt. Theodore Bennett of the Machine Gun Corps who was also killed in the war, on September 7th 1918 when attached to the Indian Infantry.

In July 1922 Paul Bennett married Miss Violet Forster who at one time had been a song writer, and they had one daughter and a son. Bennett was called to the bar at the Middle Temple in 1923 and was Prosecuting Counsel on the S. E. Circuit between 1931 and 1935 when he became a Metropolitan Magistrate, a position that he was to hold until 1961. He sat at the West London Magistrate Court for eleven years and then at the Marlborough Street Court from 1946 until 1961. He was also a Governor of the Regency Polytechnic. In the second war the Bennetts were bombed out twice in their home in Marylebone. In 1946 their only son died of pneumonia and in 1949 his wife "went missing" for a few days before being found in a distressed condition on Hampstead Heath. The Bennetts retired to Vincenza, North Italy where Paul died on April 6th 1970 at the age of 77, Violet survived him. After her husband's death sho wrote to the Headmaster of Marling School telling him that she would like the school to have a picture of her late husband that used to hang in the Marlborough Street Court. It was of Bennett in the uniform of a Squadron Leader in the R.A.F. when he had been an officer in the Air Training Corps in the Second War. The portrait was hung in the school hall. The Bennett prize for 'outstanding service to the School' was also established. Bennett's addresses in England after the Great War were 18 Manor Gardens, London, SW19 in the 1920s and later Homefield, Aldwich, Sussex. His medals are in the possession of the Worcester Regimental Museum.

On his death *The Times* described Bennett as 'Soldier and Magistrate', he excelled at both careers.

J. Cunningham

JOHN CUNNINGHAM, V.C.
EAST YORKS. REGT.

John Cunningham V.C. (Christopher Ketchell Collection, Hull)

In the time between Lt. E. P. Bennett gaining the V.C. at Le Transloy on November 5th and Pte. John Cunning-

ham winning his on November 13th the Allies had been making their final preparations for the commencement of the Battle of the Ancre.

We are not directly concerned here with the main part of the battle as Cunningham's unit the 12th East Yorks (92nd Bde.) 31st. Div. was to the north protecting the left flank of the Allied attack. The 93rd Bde. was on the left of the front line to the south east of

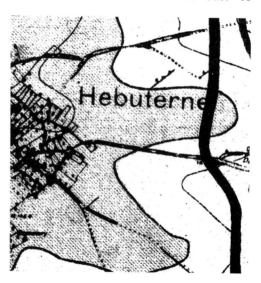

Hebuterne and the 92nd were on its right. The 92nd Bde. consisted of four battalions from the East Yorkshire Regiment, the 10th, 11th, 12th and 13th. The Brigade had been in reserve at Serre on July 1st when the rest of the Division suffered extremely high casualties but were not going to 'escape' again.

Pte. Cunningham's unit, the 12th East Yorks, together with the 13th Bn. pushed forward from their assembly positions soon after midnight on November 13th, with snipers and Lewis guns. By this early start they were to provide support on the left flank when zero hour for the battle arrived a few hours later. The Yorkshiremen reached the German front trench without any major difficulty but the enemy was in no mood to give up its support trench and fought back with rifle fire and bombs. On the right of the line the 13th Bn. had a very hard time of it and suffered very high casualties in the fighting. The attackers continued to use communication trenches that stretched as far back as Star Wood for conducting bombing counter attacks from. The British hung on to what ground they had captured but were running very short of bombs. It was during this part of the fight that Pte. Cunningham carried out his deeds that gained him a V.C. and the citation for the medal which was published on January 13th 1917 tells the story in the following manner:

"For most conspicuous bravery and resource during operations.

After the enemy's front line had been captured, Pte. Cunningham proceeded with a bombing section up a communica-

Pte. John Cunningham, V.C., East York Regt. (portrait left) in a communication-trench beyond a captured line went forward alone, and meeting ten of the enemy killed them with bombs and cleared the trench up to the next line.

Opposite Hebuterne November 13th 1916

tion trench. Much opposition was encountered, and the rest of the section became casualties. Collecting all the bombs from the casualties, this gallant soldier went on alone. Having expended all his bombs, he returned for a fresh supply and again proceeded to the communication trench, where he met a party of ten of the enemy. These he killed and cleared the trench up to the enemy line.

His conduct throughout the day was magnificent."

Hyde Park, June 2nd 1917

Later on in the day unfortunately the 3rd Division on the 31st's right were unsuccessful in their fight against the German positions at Serre, the reason being that the Germans had a very clear field of view over their attackers. This situation led to an exposed flank which could only be cured by the retreat to its own lines of the 92nd Bde. The very great sacrifice of the East Yorkshire Battalions on the 13th of November 1916 have tended to be obscured by the relative progress in the day further south and especially at Beaumont Hamel, Beaucourt and St. Pierre Divion.

Cunningham was awarded his V.C by the King at a ceremony in Hyde Park on June 2nd 1917.

John Cunningham who was usually known as Jack was the son of Charles Cunningham, a licensed hawker and of his wife Mary Ann. John was born on June 28th 1897 at Swaby's Yard, Scunthorpe, which no longer exists. The family later moved to Hull and John attended schools at St James Day School, Wheeler Street (later Newington High) and Chiltern Street School. The original Chiltern School has been pulled down and a modern primary school built in its place. The family lived at Edgar Street, Hessle Road, behind St. James, Hull, which has now been redeveloped. His education was often interrupted as his parents were often on the move.

After he left school John became a hawker, like his father before him and then he enlisted with the 3rd. Hull Battalion in 1915 when he was seventeen. He carried out his initial army training at South Dalton near Beverley and later served with the East Yorks in Egypt from December 1915 to March 1916, when their role was to guard the Suez Canal.

Wheeler Street School, Hull (D. G. Woodhouse)

They then moved to France and the Western Front. On June 2nd 1917 he was one of 350 men and women to be decorated at a special public ceremony of investiture that took place at Hyde Park. It was a beautiful summer's day and aircraft of the Royal Flying Corps patrolled the skies overhead in case of a surprise attack by German Gotha Bombers. A Guards Brigade provided suitable music for the occasion. The ceremony was also filmed. Cunningham was one of the first men to be decorated by the King and the other early recipients included several other Somme V.C. winners, Hughes, White, Allen, and Bradford. The crowd were able to follow the presentation by reference to a programme. Each man or woman had a number and this number was displayed on boards in various parts of the crowd. This way everyone present knew who was who. It was interesting that owing to superstition the number 13 was dropped from the proceedings. Roland Bradford was number 14 in the list instead of 13 but the altering of his number did not prevent him from being killed by a stray shell nearly six months later. When Cunningham's turn came to be paraded in front of the King there was a roar from the crowd who had read of his deed in their programmes. The King talked to the 'Hull Hero' for some little time. The last people who were decorated were members of the nursing profession and they were followed by the families of those who had won their awards posthumously.

Later that evening, Cunningham left London with his parents who had also been present at the reception at Hyde Park, to return home to Hull for leave and the city was to give him a huge welcome. Although his train arrived at Paragon Station at 2 o'clock on a Sunday morning the crowds were there waiting to greet their 'local hero'. On emerging from the station, at the former Anlaby Road entrance a great roar went up and he was immediately hoisted shoulder high and carried home. During the same leave he visited St James School and although later there were plans to erect a plaque to Cunningham at Wheeler Street School, they were not carried through. The local cinema, the Hull Palace showed the film of the investiture that had taken place at Hyde Park at 'both houses' while Cunningham was on leave.

John Cunningham, his parents and a younger brother were also invited to be guests at a crowded meeting of Hull City Council at the Guildhall, where he was given an official welcome on behalf of the City and also presented with an Illuminated Address. Cunningham gave a short message of thanks and was applauded continuously. In his remarks the Lord Mayor, Alderman F. Askew said this to Cunningham in his public address:

". . . It was open to him, as well as to any of the rank and file, not only in the Army, but in civil life, by his zeal, industry, and determination, to achieve higher honours in the future. There was no doubt that his deed would be talked of for many years to come. . . ."

Cunningham was quite badly wounded in the latter part of the war and was demobilized in 1919. In the same year he married Eva Harrison who gave birth to a daughter. Shortly after his return from the Army it appears that Cunningham was having difficulty in settling down and fitting in with civilian life. As early as July 1919 we find him being summoned for physically abusing and beating up his wife. In defence he maintained that 'she left him three times a week'. The local magistrate granted Mrs Cunningham a separation order with a weekly allowance

John Cunningham 1929

of 25 shillings per week. At his appearance in court Cunningham wore his V.C. Summoned again nearly sixteen months later (November 1920) Cunningham was ordered once more to pay his wife a maintenance grant. Cunningham, who was again sporting his V.C. medal, said in his defence that he only had an income of an Army pension of £2 a week. He received this pension for being wounded in both legs and in the lungs. However these wounds did not prevent him from being involved in a brawl with an ex-soldier a couple of weeks later when he was put on remand for hitting the man on the head with a bottle.

In March 1922 Cunningham became the first of the Somme V.C. holders to be

Cunningham's parents' grave Western Cemetery, Hull (D. G. Woodhouse)

name is mentioned however on his parents' memorial stone, nearby. His medals are in the possession of the Prince of Wales' Regimental Museum. Like most V.C. winners his obituary was published in *The Times*.

Cunningham was the first man connected with Hull to win the V.C. in the Great War and he was one of four members of the East Yorkshire Regiment to receive the nation's highest military honour. In view of it now being fifty years since Cunningham's death and the end of what appeared to be a fairly tragic post war life it would seem high time for the people of Hull to commemorate their former hero. After all enough fuss was made of him when he returned home in 1917, having brought glory on himself, his regiment and his home town. It would be nice to think that Cunningham's misdemeanours could be forgiven and that at the very least a fund opened that would provide enough money for the erection of a memorial stone on his grave.

sent to prison, for failing again to keep up payments to his wife. The arrears amounted to £10. Seven years later, in November 1929 Cunningham once again made the local headlines in Hull. This time he was the victim of two fellow hawkers who had made off with his share of the value of a quantity of lino that the three had agreed to sell and split the proceeds three ways. Cunningham was not in court on this occasion as he had a more pressing engagement with the Prince of Wales at a dinner for Victoria Cross winners!

John Cunningham died at 5 Beaufort Terrace, Hull on February 21st 1941, he was only 43 years of age and had been ill for some time. This building like most in Hull associated with Cunningham has disappeared. He was buried three days later at the Western Cemetery in a grave that is unmarked but in section 181. His

John Cunningham's unmarked burial plot Western Cemetery, Hull (D. G. Woodhouse)

B. C. Freyberg

Capt. Temp. Lt.-Col.) BERNARD CYRIL FREYBERG, D.S.O., V.C

Photo : Central Press

Gallahers Cigarette Card

While John Cunningham was winning a V.C. opposite Hebuterne on November 13th the 63rd (Royal Naval) Div. were making great progress to the south east in their attempt to capture the German held village of Beaucourt. It was for his outstanding leadership on this day as commanding officer of the Hood Battalion (189th Bde.) that Lt. Col. Bernard Freyberg was to win a Victoria Cross. He had already gained a D.S.O. at Gallipoli.

The start of the Battle of the Ancre had been delayed several times because of adverse weather conditions and finally it was confirmed that it should take place on November 13th. The plan of attack was the line Serre-Beaumont Hamel-Beaucourt-St. Pierre Divion. These strongpoints were to be attacked by the 3rd, 51st and 63rd (R.N.) Divisions of Xlll Corps in the order left to right. The 63rd Div. was allotted a front that measured 1200 yards, and their right flank was on the north side of the River Ancre which ran in an easterly direction from the village of Beaucourt.

The 63rd Div. were to reach Beaucourt, their objective was to take the intervening positions. Their jumping off trenches ran in a north south line. The enemy which was nearly 250 yards away had three lines of trenches, the first line to be captured was called the 'Dotted Green Line'. Behind it was a valley which ran through the Beaucourt Station Road.

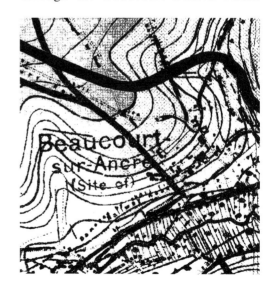

Behind this was a ridge that ran from Beaumont Hamel to the Station at Beaucourt, this line was called the 'Green Line', and ran down as far as the Ancre river. The third objective was called the 'Yellow Line'and was in front of Beaucourt village. The village itself was to be the final objective and was known as the 'Red Line.'

The Hood, Hawke, Howe and lst Royal Marines from the 189th and 190th Brigades moved off first at 5.45 am, it was not only pitch dark but there was a Scotch mist as well. They were to capture the first three German lines and then consolidate on the third objective. From the start the situation was confused and the attacking units quickly became inter mixed. In the mist the Drake Battalion got too far ahead of the advance and they hadn't even noticed the enemy lines, although they had bombed several German dug-outs. They also found themselves too close to their own barrage and lost some men as a result. At the line above Station Road, as it was at last getting light, Freyberg assumed command of the operation. He had been commander of the Hood Battalion and was dressed in his 'number one rig', he was an imposing sight on the battlefield being over six feet tall and weighing sixteen stone. Chief Petty Officer Tobin later recalled the following greeting from Freyberg:

"Hullo, Tobin, I think we will get a V.C. today."

This was after Freyberg's Adjutant and Signals Officer had both been killed on either side of him. At the 'Yellow Line' in front of Beaucourt Freyberg gave instructions to dig two lines of trenches while the attack on the village was organised. At this time the British Artillery were again causing casualties by 'dropping short'. In

Beaucourt-sur-Ancre November 13th 1916

addition German snipers in front of Beaucourt were very active and causing casualties with their accurate rifle fire. However the trenches gave the attackers some protection. Here they dug in for the night which was a very cold one, while the British bombardment continued until the situation on the left flank was more clear. At 6a.m. on the 14th the 190th Bde. (R.N.D.) was to attack and become level with the Naval Division's advance and then at 7.45 a.m. the Brigade was to attack and capture Beaucourt. The German machine gunners and snipers were very active and the Allied barrage ineffectual. At zero hour Freyberg, disregarding any risk to his own life climbed out of his trench and led the attack in person. The first wave stopped three times and at this time Freyberg was knocked over by a bullet which hit his helmet. He scrambled up again and went on into Beaucourt with the Royal Naval Division behind him. The Germans decided not to make a fight of it and surrendered in their hundreds. They came out of their holes, tore off their equipment and gave themselves up. After the village was captured it was decided to make a trench on the far side of the village. At this stage the German snipers were still firing very accurately and although wounded Freyberg was able to carry on with his duties of organising the battle. This was just before 9 a.m. and suddenly the German heavy guns started firing into the village. Conditions for the Marines became very hazardous and unfortunately their commanding officer Lt. Col. Freyberg was hit for the third time but this time much more seriously. His wound, which was in his neck, was bleeding profusely and was dressed by The Hon. Lionel S. Montagu a brother officer who also gave Freyberg some morphia. After about ten minutes the shelling eased and Montagu suggested that he should get three men to take him down the line for medical treatment. Freyberg, who was still giving instructions despite his wounds would not hear of such a suggestion and then asked Montagu if he would walk him down to the aid post. The distance was 300 yards and Freyberg lent on his colleague for support as they negotiated the German shelling and the various shell holes in their path. The regimental aid post was in the shelter of a bank where members of the Drake and Hood battalions were sheltering as were a number of staff officers, according to Montagu. Freyberg was immediately administered to by the Regimental Doctor and gave instructions for the commander of the 13th K.R.R.C. to take over from him.

It is hardly surprising that after being

wounded three times in the same action and of almost leading the attack on Beaucourt single handed that Freyberg should be granted the V.C. The citation was published very soon afterwards on December 15th 1916 and read as follows:

"For most conspicuous bravery and brilliant leading as a Battalion Commander.

By his splendid personal gallantry he carried the initial attack straight through the enemy's front system of trenches. Owing to mist and heavy fire of all descriptions, Lieutenant-Colonel Freyberg's command was much disorganised after the capture of the first objective. He personally rallied and re-formed his men, including men from other units who had become intermixed.

He inspired all with his own contempt of danger. At the appointed time he led his men to the successful assault of the second objective, many prisoners being captured.

During this advance he was twice wounded. He again rallied and re-formed all who were with him, and although unsupported in a very advanced position, he held his ground for the remainder of the day, and throughout the night, under heavy artillery and machine gun fire. When reinforced on the following morning, he organised the attack on a strongly fortified village and showed a fine example of dash in personally leading the assault, capturing the village and five hundred prisoners. In this operation he was again wounded.

Later in the afternoon, he was again wounded severely, but refused to leave the line till he had issued final instructions.

The personality, valour and utter contempt of danger on the part of this single Officer enabled the lodgment in

St Martha's Church, Chilworth, Surrey (W. Marsh)

the most advanced objective of the Corps to be permanently held, and on this point d'appui the line was eventually formed."

Freyberg was the last man to be awarded the V.C. during the battle of the Somme but not the last man to have his citation published. The citation for George Evans was not published until 1920.

The battle of the Somme officially finished on November 18th. As we have seen Beaucourt fell on the 14th and the British were able to advance to the north and south of the Ancre and reach the outskirts of Grandcourt. Freyberg did not collect his V.C. from the King at Buckingham Palace until January 2nd 1918.

———

Bernard Cyril Freyberg was born in Richmond, Surrey on March 21st 1889.

He was the seventh son of James Freyberg and the fifth by his second wife Julia Hamilton. The family left for New Zealand in 1891 and settled in Wellington. Bernard was educated at Wellington College and was to become an excellent swimmer. He had ambitions to swim the English Channel. In Otago he qualified as a dentist in 1911 and also joined the Territorials. He was gazetted as a 2nd Lieutenant in 1912. In 1913 he took on the job of a ship's stoker and sailed to Sydney. On returning home he obtained a stoker's certificate and sailed to America.

Freyberg's ability for being in the right place at the right time now began to operate, as in August 1914, on the outbreak of war he found himself in London. Not only that but somehow he wangled an interview with Winston

Churchill who obviously liked him as he procured for him a position with the Hood Battalion of the Royal Naval Division. He was sent with the Division on an ill fated expedition to Antwerp, which was one of Churchill's brain-childs and managed to escape with his company via Ostend by sea.

On February 28th 1915 Freyberg sailed with the Hood battalion of the R.N.D. to Gallipoli. His officers' mess at this time included Alan Herbert, Rupert Brooke and Arthur Asquith, son of the Prime Minister. When Brooke died of blood poisoning Freyberg was one of the pall-bearers on the Island of Skyros on April 23rd 1915. The role of the R.N.D. was to cover the landings and at one time Freyberg's swimming prowess came in very useful as he swam ashore to the Gulf of Xeros where he lit a series of flares on the beach, thus simulating a landing. He got back safely to his ship and not surprisingly was later awarded the D.S.O. for his boldness.

In July Freyberg was wounded but recovered quickly and was made commanding officer of the Hood Battalion, and returned to England in January 1916 after the evacuation of the Peninsula. The R.N.D. was reformed as the 63rd R.N.D. and sailed for France in May 1916. Freyberg was now Lieutenant-Colonel. His wounds in the November Somme battle took several months to heal and he was not fit until March 1917. He was promoted to the rank of Brigadier-General in command of 173rd Bde (58th Div). He fought with them at Bullecourt and in September in the third battle of Ypres, where he was again seriously wounded. After three months he returned to Passchendaele, as commander of the 88th Bde. (29th Div.). He won two bars to his D.S.O. during the remaining months of the war and ended it having been wounded six times. The French also gave him a medal, the Croix de Guerre with palms. In addition his name had also been mentioned in despatches several times.

I have dealt at length with Freyberg's record during the Great War because apart from Carton de Wiart he was surely the greatest soldier who was to be a winner of the Victoria Cross during the battle of the Somme?

I will pass quickly over the rest of Freyberg's career but suffice to say that he brought to bear all his unique qualities to any job or position that he was offered. After the war he flirted briefly with politics, took a staff course at Sandhurst, served briefly with the Grenadier Guards and the Manchester Regiment and made three attempts to swim the English Channel. In the 1930's he became a senior officer in Southern Command and

St Martha's Churchyard, Chilworth, Surrey (W. Marsh)

was made up to a Major-General. In 1937 he was declared medically unfit and left the Army and gained a position with B.S.A., he also dabbled again with politics and was adopted as a prospective Conservative candidate.

In 1939 he was recalled to the Army and took command of the New Zealand Army and was with them in North Africa. Before then he had an unusual setback when in Command of the Island of Crete he and his troops were lucky to escape from the German airborne landing. The enemy was infinitely better equipped for the task of holding the island.

As a result of his very close ties with New Zealand Freyberg became its Governor General after the war until 1952. He then returned to England and became Lieutenant Governor of Windsor Castle.

Freyberg was to receive many military and civil honours and was awarded a 3rd Bar to his D.S.O. in Italy for the advance on Trieste in 1945. He was appointed K.B.E. in 1942 and G.C.M.G. in 1946. In 1951 he was created 1st Baron of Wellington, New Zealand, and of Munstead in the county of Surrey. In 1922 he had married Barbara Jekyll and they had one son, Paul Richard, born in 1923. Lady Freyberg who was involved in troop welfare and received an O.B.E., was as popular as her husband in New Zealand.

Bernard Freyberg died at Windsor on July 4th 1963, at the age of 74, where he had been the Governor of the Castle since 1952. He is burried at St. Martha's churchyard, Chilworth, Surrey. Freyberg's wife lived on until 1973 and their son succeeded to the Peerage. In commemoration of this brilliant soldier and administrator there is a bust of his likeness in the Guildhall London. In the crypt of St. Paul's there is a bronze of him designed by Nemon in the Soldier's Corner. There is also a commemoration of him in St. George's Chapel, Windsor. His medals are in private hands.

Bibliography

The London Gazette 1916–1920

The Lummis Files in the care of the Military Historical Society at the National Army Museum

Sir O'Moore Creagh V.C. and Miss E. M. Humphris The V.C. and D.S.O. 1924.

The Register of the Victoria Cross – This England Books. 1988

W. Alister Williams – The VCs of Wales and the Welsh Regiments. 1984

Sir John Smyth VC – The Story of the Victoria Cross. 1963

The Times

The Daily Telegraph

Lancashire Evening Post

Yorkshire Post

Yorkshire Evening News

A Memoir and some letters of Frank Maxwell, V.C. 1921

J. W. Bancroft – The Victoria Cross Roll of Honour. 1988

H. L. Kirby & R. R. Walsh – The Seven V.C.s of Stonyhurst College. 1987

The Medical Victoria Crosses, n.d.

N. McCrery – For Conspicuous Gallantry A Brief History of the Recipients of the Victoria Cross from Nottinghamshire and Derbyshire

J. W. Bancroft – Devotion to Duty – Tributes to a Region's V.C.s 1990

B. Clark – The Victoria Cross: a Register of Awards to Irish-born Officers and men, The Irish Sword. 1986

G. Gliddon – When the Barrage Lifts – A topographical history and commentary on the Battle of the Somme 1916. 1987

C. H. Dudley Ward, D.S.O., M.C. – Regimental Records of the Royal Welch Fusiliers (23rd Foot). 1928

Memorials of Rugbeians Who Fell in the Great War, Volume 3. 1917

C. E. W. Bean – The Official History of Australia in the War of 1914–1918 Volume 3, The A.I.F. in France 1916. 1929

Lt.Gen. Sir A. Carton de Wiart – Happy Odyssey The Memoirs of . . . 1950

C. Falls – The History of the 36th (Ulster) Division. 1922

L. Wigmore & B. Harding – They Dared Mightily. 1963

S. Gummer – The Chavasse Twins. 1963

T. Norman, ed. Armageddon Road – A VC's Diary 1914–16. 1982

L. Macdonald – Somme. 1983

M. Middlebrook – The First Day on the Somme 1 July 1916. 1971

I. Uys – For Valour, the History of Southern Africa's Victoria Cross Heroes. 1973

I. Uys – Delville Wood. 1983

P. Orr – The Road to the Somme, Men of the Ulster Division Tell Their Story. 1987

Sir J. E. Edmonds (ed) Military Operations France and Belgium. 1922–1949

Thirty Canadian V.C.'s. 1918

H. M. Urquart – History of the 16th Battalion – The Canadian Scottish-Canadian Expeditionary Force in the Great War. 1933

A. F. Duguid – Official History of the Canadian Forces in the Great War, 1914–1919. 1938

Appendices

Additional sources:
E. N. F. Bell
Sir F. Fox – The Royal Inniskilling
  Fusiliers in the Great War. 1928
G. S. Cather
Memorials of Rugbeians Who Fell in the
  Great War Volume III. 1917
Hazelwood School, Limpsfield
English Heroes (This England Summer
  1986)
A. R. Burrows – The Royal Irish
  Fusiliers. 1927
J. L. Green
Commonwealth War Graves Commis-
  sion
Coin and Medal News
Hunts Post
Contemporary Biographies of Hunts
S. W. Loudoun-Shand
The Legion (July/August 1986)
H. C. Wylly – The Green Howards in the
  Great War. 1926
W. F. McFadzean
Belfast Telegraph
Royal Ulster Rifles Association
R. Quigg
Belfast Telegraph
Northern Constitutional
Daily Mail
W. Ritchie
War Diary of the 2nd Bn. Seaforth
  Highlanders
Cabar Feidh
Glasgow Evening Times
R. H. Q. Queen's Own Highlanders
Major Gen. Sir John Laurie experiences
  as Adjutant of the 2nd Bn. Seaforth
  Highlanders 1916 (I.W.M.)
G. Sanders

Yorkshire Evening Post
Yorkshire Evening News
This England
E. Wyrall – The West Yorkshire Regim-
  ent in the War, 1914–1918. 1924
J. Y. Turnbull
The Royal Highland Fusiliers
The Outpost (December 1916)
Glasgow Herald
L. B. Oatts – Proud Heritage. The Story
  of the Highland Light Infantry Vol 3.
  1961
A. Carton de Wiart
Lady Joan Carton de Wiart
Dictionary of National Bibliography
  1961–1970. 1981
Daily Sketch
Evening News
The Sunday Times
The Times
Daily Telegraph
Back Badge (1966)
E. Wyrall – History of the 19th Division,
  1914–1918. 1921
T. G. Turrall
Commonwealth War Graves Commis-
  sion
Worcestershire Regimental Museum
Dennis Gillard
"Firm"
H. F. Stacke – The Worcestershire
  Regiment in the Great War. 1929
T. O. L. Wilkinson
The Sphere
The Regimental Association The Loyal
  Regiment (North Lancashire)
H. C. Wylly – The Loyal North Lan-
  cashire Regiment. 1933
D. S. Bell

Yorkshire Evening Post
H. C. Wylly – The Green Howards in the
    Great War. 1926
W. F. Boulter
Leicester Mercury
Sir Ivor Maxse – Notes on the Somme
    Situation July 11th 1916
Irene Progin
R. Gurney – History of the North-
    amptonshire Regiment, 1742–1934.
    1935
W. F. Faulds
S. Monick – W. F. Faulds, VC, MC: A
    Uniquely South African Victoria Cross
    Group (Museum Review Vol 1 No 6,
    September 1987)
South African Museum of Military His-
    tory
East Anglian Daily Times
W. La T. Congreve
Royal Green Jackets Museum
Dennis Gillard
Country Life 1916
Daily Mirror
Daily Telegraph
The Guardian
Sunday Express
Cheshire Express
The Rifle Brigade Chronicle 1916
The Suffolk Regimental Gazette (April
    1926)
J. Fellows – For Valour – Wirral Family's
    Double Distinction (1966)
H. G. Parkyn – A Short History of The
    Rifle Brigade. 1922
J. J. Davies
The Times History and Encyclopaedia of
    the War
Bournemouth Evening Echo
A. Hill
North Cheshire Herald and Hyde Repor-
    ter
T. W. H. Veale
Evening Standard

Brenda Ward
Western Morning News
C. T. Atkinson – The Devonshire
    Regiment, 1914–1918. 1926
Devonshire and Dorset Regimental Jour-
    nal
The Devonshire and Dorset Regiment
J. Leak
Australian War Memorial Canberra
Dictionary of Australian National Biog-
    raphy
A. S. Blackburn
Dictionary of Australian National Biog-
    raphy
Australian War Memorial Canberra
10th Bn. A.I.F. War Diary
T. Cooke
Australian War Memorial Canberra
Dictionary of Australian National Biog-
    raphy
G. Bryant – Where the Prize is Highest:
    The Stories of the New Zealanders
    Who Won the Victoria Cross. 1972
A. Gill
Evening News
C. C. Castleton
Australian War Memorial Canberra
K. W. Mackenzie – The Story of the 17th
    Bn, A.I.F. in the Great War. 1946
Lowestoft Journal
W. J. G. Evans
The Croydon Times and Advertiser
The Child's Guardian
Tameside Metropolitan Borough Coun-
    cil
The Manchester Museum Committee of
    the King's Regiment
Sixteenth; Seventeenth; Eighteenth;
    Nineteenth Battalions The Manchester
    Regiment (First City Brigade). A
    Record 1914–1918. 1923
J. Miller
Lancaster City Council
Lancaster Evening Post

J. M. Garwood

W. H. Short

H. C. Wylly – The Green Howards in the Great War, 1926

G. G. Coury

The Stonyhurst Magazine

The South Lancashire Regiment Newsletter

The Liverpool Echo

The Warrington Guardian

Yorkshire Evening News

B. R. Mullaly – The South Lancashire Regiment The Prince of Wales' Volunteers. n.d.

H. Whalley-Kelly – "Ich Dien" The Prince of Wales' Volunteers (South Lancashire) 1914–1934. 1935

N. G. Chavasse

Mrs Ann Clayton

D. Cargill – Serving the Outpatients in Hell (Medical. Jan 1981)

Liverpool Daily Post

This England

Daily Mail

M. O'Meara

Australian War Memorial Canberra

The West Australian

Australian Dictionary of Biography

W. B. Allen

Edinburgh Evening News

Daily Mail

Chichester Observer

The Star (Sheffield)

Yesterday No 22 February 1990

T. Hughes

The Star

Daily Telegraph

J. V. Holland

The Mercury (Tasmania)

Clongowes College School Magazine

S. Lindsay – Merseyside Heroes (unpublished ms)

D. Jones

National Museums and Galleries on Merseyside

Liverpool Echo

S. Lindsay – Merseyside Heroes (unpublished ms)

L. Clarke

Department of Public Records and Archives, Toronto

W. W. Murray – The History of the 2nd Canadian Battalion. n.d.

D. F. Brown

Auckland Institute and Museum

G. Bryant – Where the Prize is Highest The Stories of the New Zealanders who won the Victoria Cross. 1972

Sanders, J. New Zealand VC Winners. 1974

Official History of the Otago Regt. in the Great War by Lt. A. E. Byrne, MC. n.d.

F. McNess

Yorkshire Evening Post

Yorkshire Post

Bournemouth Daily Echo

The Scots Guards

J. V. Campbell

Punch. 1916

W. Oliver Wicks

Daily Mail

Gloucestershire Gazette

L. Pearce – V.C.s of the Coldstream Guards

J. F. G. Ross-of-Bladenberg – The Coldstream Guards, 1914–1918. 1926

J. C. Kerr

Canadian Official History

National Archives of Canada

T. A. Jones

Runcorn Guardian

Runcorn Weekly News

Wide World Magazine

Cheshire Chronicle

The Oak Tree, the Cheshire Regimental Journal

A. Crookenden – The History of the Cheshire Regimen in the Great War. 1939

F. J. Edwards and R. E. Ryder
Star and Garter News
Soldier
The Die-hards (Middlesex Regimental
  Journal)
Middlesex Regimental Museum
The Sunday Express
E. Wyrall – The Die-Hards in the Great
  War, 1914–1918. (1926–1930)
T. E. Adlam
Public Record Office
G. H. F. Nicholls – The 18th Division in
  the Great War. 1922
D. A. B. Shardlow interview with
  daughter Mrs J. Swinstead, November
  1990
Luton Museum and Art Gallery
Frank Maxwell V.C.
A.C.T. White
Yorkshire Evening Post
The Green Howards Gazette
Regimental HQ the Green Howards
R. B. Bradford
Jack Cavanagh
Brig.-Gen. R. B. Bradford VC, MC and
  His Brothers, privately published, n.d.
R. Bradford – The Attack made by the
  50th Division on the Butte-de-
  Warlencourt and the Gird Line on
  November 5th 1916 (S. Shannon
  D.L.I. Museum)
H. Kelly
Daily Herald
The Duke of Wellington's Regiment
The Iron Duke
E. Wyrall – The West Yorkshire Regim-
  ent in the War, 1914–1918. 1924
10th Bn The Duke of Wellington's
  Regiment War Diary

J. C. Richardson
Directorate of National Defence Canada
D. A. Melville – Canadians and the
  Victoria Cross. n.d.
H. M. Urquart – History of the 16th Bn. –
  The Canadian Scottish-Canadian Ex-
  peditionary Force in the Great War.
  1933
National Archives of Canada
R. Downie
Glasgow Evening Herald
E. P. Bennett
W. Oliver Wicks – History of Marling
  School
Stroud and the Great War 1914–1919
Daily Mail
H. F. Stacke – The Worcestershire
  Regiment in the Great War. 1929
J. Cunningham
D. G. Woodhouse
Hull Daily Mail
Grimsby Daily Telegraph
Eastern Morning News
The Sapper
S. Kimberley – Humberside in the First
  World War, n.d.
B. C. Freyberg
Royal Marines Museum
Dictionary of National Biography 1961–
  1970. 1981
Major, the Hon. Lionel S. Montagu
  R.M.L.I. letter to his mother dated
  November 20th 1916 Arch 11/12/13
  (33) R.M.L.I. Museum
D. Jerrold The Royal Naval Division.
  1923
H. E. Blumberg – Royal Marines in the
  War of 1914–1919, n.d.
W. J. Marsh